NEW MAPS OF HELL

NEW MAPS OF HELL

A Survey of Science Fiction

BY KINGSLEY AMIS

HARCOURT, BRACE AND
COMPANY · NEW YORK

© 1960 by Kingsley Amis

C.9.60

Library of Congress Catalog Card Number: 60-5441
Printed in the United States of America

To Bruce Montgomery

FOREWORD

I have been a devotee of science fiction ever since investigating, at the age of twelve or so, a bin in the neighbourhood Woolworth's with the label YANK MAGAZINES: *Interesting Reading*. Those stories of twenty-five years ago, of course, with their exploitation of violence and horror, were as far below the level of contemporary science fiction as the music of the B.B.C. Dance Orchestra (which provided another key epiphany of that period) was below that of Louis Armstrong's Hot Five; but the first coverful of many-eyed and -tentacled monsters was enough assurance for me, as it must have been for thousands of others, that this was the right kind of stuff. This strongly suggests, at least, that what attracts people to science fiction is not in the first place literary quality in the accustomed sense of that term. But, as I shall argue in what is to follow, they may well come to find such quality there, perhaps in an unaccustomed form, if they ever take the trouble to look for it. This book is offered in the belief that to read, and to study, science fiction are valid and interesting pursuits from any old point of view, whether literary, sociological, psychological, political, or what you will, though the first of these will probably keep you going longer than any of the others.

I gave the history of my early conversion not merely for

its intrinsic enchantment, but to reassure any regular science-fiction reader who may pick up this book that, whatever my shortcomings, I am not that peculiarly irritating kind of person, the intellectual who takes a slumming holiday in order to "place" some "phenomenon" of "popular culture"; one recalls with aversion those attempts to "place" jazz by academic musicians who thought Duke Ellington's band was a kind of minstrel troupe. On the other hand, I am not a professional editor or critic of science fiction nor, as yet, a habitual writer of it. This deficiency gives me some freedom of manoeuvre in a field in which— let us face the fact—there is at present a discreditable provincialism of thought and too much nervous or complacent reluctance to invoke ordinary critical standards. Science fiction is not tomfool sensationalism, but neither is it a massive body of serious art destined any moment to engulf the whole of Anglo-American writing.

The text here printed bears a strong resemblance to a series of lectures delivered by me in the spring of 1959 as part of the 1958-59 programme of the Christian Gauss Seminars in Criticism at Princeton University. My appreciative thanks are due to the members of the Seminar Committee, and in particular to its chairman, Professor R. P. Blackmur, for his constant support and encouragement in my presentation of a topic initially unfamiliar to him; to Professor Serge Sobolevitch, Mr. Alan Williams, Mr. Ian Ballantine, Mr. Mark Rose, and Mr. Edmund Crispin for much generous help, both practical and verbal; and to Mrs. Stewart Richardson, who got the manuscript into publishable form and made many valuable suggestions.

CONTENTS

What makes us rove that starlit corridor
May be the impulse to meet face to face
Our vice and folly shaped into a thing,
And so at last ourselves; what lures us there
Is simpler versions of disaster:
A web confounding time and space,
A world of ocean without shore,
A sentence to perpetual journeying,
And simplest, flapping down the poisoned air,
A ten-clawed monster.

In him, perhaps, we see the general ogre
Who rode our ancestors to nightmare,
And in his habitat their maps of hell.
But climates and geographies soon change,
Spawning mutations none can quell
With silver sword or necromancer's ring,
Worse than their sires, more durable,
And of a wider range.

I · STARTING POINTS ▶

Those who have never seen a living Martian can scarcely imagine the strange horror of its appearance. The peculiar V-shaped mouth with its pointed upper lip, the absence of brow ridges, the absence of a chin beneath the wedge-like lower lip, the incessant quivering of this mouth, the Gorgon groups of tentacles, the tumultuous breathing of the lungs in a strange atmosphere, the evident heaviness and painfulness of movement due to the greater gravitational energy of the earth—above all, the extraordinary intensity of the immense eyes—were at once vital, intense, inhuman, crippled and monstrous. There was something fungoid in the oily brown skin, something in the clumsy deliberation of the tedious movements unspeakably nasty. Even at this first encounter, this first glimpse, I was overcome with disgust and dread.

If that produces no special reaction—it comes, of course, from an early chapter of *The War of the Worlds*—perhaps this passage will:

"I don't have to tell you men that Point-of-Sale has its special problems," Harvey said, puffing his thin cheeks. "I swear, the whole damned Government must be infiltrated with [Conservationists]! You know what they've done. They outlawed compulsive subsonics in our aural advertising—but we've bounced back with a list of semantic cue words that tie in with every basic trauma and neurosis in American life today. They listened to the safety cranks and stopped us from projecting our messages on aircar windows—but we bounced back. Lab tells me," he nodded to our Director of Research across the table, "that soon we'll be testing a system that projects direct on the retina of the eye. . . ." He broke off, "Excuse me, Mr. Schocken," he whispered. "Has Security checked this room?"

Fowler Schocken nodded. "Absolutely clean. Nothing but the usual State Department and House of Representatives spy-mikes. And of course we're feeding a canned playback into them."

I quote that extract from *The Space Merchants* (a novel published in 1953) and the H. G. Wells piece in order to make possible a tiny experiment in self-analysis: anybody encountering such passages who fails to experience a peculiar interest, related to, but distinct from, ordinary literary interest, will never be an addict of science fiction. Now I acknowledge that people can live out happy and useful lives in complete indifference to this form of writing, but the point about addiction is the one where investigation should start. Those who decide that they ought to "find out about" science fiction, suspecting that it furnishes a new vantage point from which to survey "our culture," will find much to confirm that suspicion and also, I hope, much incidental entertainment, but they are unlikely to be able to share, nor even perhaps to comprehend, the experience of the addicts, who form the overwhelming majority of science-fiction readers, and to whom, naturally, entertainment is not incidental but essential. As is the way with addictions, this one is mostly contracted in adolescence or not at all, like addiction to jazz. The two have much in common, and their actual coexistence in the same person is not unusual.

The two modes themselves, indeed, show marked similarities. Both emerged as self-contained entities some time in the second or third decade of the century, and both, far more precisely, underwent rapid internal change around

1940. Both have strong connections with what I might call mass culture without being, as I hope to show in the case of science fiction, mass media in themselves. Both are characteristically American* products with a large audience and a growing band of practitioners in Western Europe, excluding the Iberian peninsula and, probably, Ireland. Both in their different ways have a noticeably radical tinge, showing itself again and again in the content of science fiction, while as regards jazz, whose material is perforce non-political, radicalism of some sort often appears in the attitudes of those connected with it; a recent article in the *Spectator* claimed that one might as well give up hope of meeting a British intellectual committed to jazz who was not firmly over to the left in politics. Both of these fields, again, have thrown up a large number of interesting and competent figures without producing anybody of first-rate importance; both have arrived at a state of anxious and largely naïve self-consciousness; both, having decisively and for something like half a century separated themselves from the main streams of serious music and serious literature, show signs of bending back towards those streams. One shouldn't go on like this all night; the two forms have no helpful resemblance, for example, in origin or in role, but I should like to round off this catalogue of supposed parallels by observing that both jazz and science fiction have in the last dozen years begun to attract the attention of the cultural diagnostician, or trend-hound, who becomes

* The prehistory of science fiction, up until 1914 or later, is admittedly as much British as American, and until quite recently the phenomenon of the serious author who takes an occasional trip into science fiction (Huxley, Orwell, William Golding—in a rather different sense) has been British rather than American. But the general run is so firmly American that British science-fiction writers will often fabricate American backgrounds and fill their dialogue with what they believe to be American idioms. (Compare the British "tough" thriller, at any rate on its lower levels.)

interested in them not for or as themselves, but for the light they can be made to throw on some other thing. By saying this I mean only to distinguish this interest, not to denigrate it; it seems worthy enough, even praiseworthy.

A definition of science fiction, though attempted with enormous and significant frequency by commentators inside the field, is bound to be cumbersome rather than memorable. With the "fiction" part we are on reasonably secure ground; the "science" part raises several kinds of difficulty, one of which is that science fiction is not necessarily fiction about science or scientists, nor is science necessarily important in it. Prolonged cogitation, however, would lead one to something like this: Science fiction is that class of prose narrative treating of a situation that could not arise in the world we know, but which is hypothesised on the basis of some innovation in science or technology, or pseudo-science or pseudo-technology, whether human or extra-terrestrial in origin. This is the kind of definition that demands footnotes. "Prose narrative," then, because the appearance of science-fiction interests in verse form have so far been of minor extent. An occasional dreadful poem about the majesty of the stars and so on struggles into one or another of the magazines as a page-filler, and there is in England a poet of some standing, Robert Conquest, whose works include an ode to the first explorers of Mars and a report on Terran culture imagined as the work of a survey team constituted by the headquarters of the Galactic Federation (plus a whole science-fiction novel, *A World of Difference*). But Conquest is at the moment a rather lonely figure, or perhaps a pioneer. I draw attention also to the existence of a volume called *The Space Child's Mother Goose*, which contains ingenious, but not always striking, variations on nursery rhymes—"This is the theory that Jack built," and so on—with contemporary *art-nouveau* illustrations. The work falls into that category of adults' children's books which has so far unaccountably eluded the trend-hounds (unless I have missed something, which I well may), and although the volume got a review in *Astounding Science Fiction*, rather puzzled in tone, I doubt if it has much circulation among ordinary readers of that journal.

To hark back now to my definition: its crucial point, clearly, lies in the mention of science and technology and their pseudo-forms. Many stories are based on, or incidentally involve, perfectly plausible extensions of existing theories and techniques. The use of robots, for instance, still a very popular subject, seems actually foreseeable, however unlikely, and even if the problem of fitting all that machinery into a container on the human scale would require the development of a kind of micro-electronics that for the time being, one would imagine, is at a rudimentary stage. Stories based on, or involving, space flight, again, which form probably the largest class, can rest on principles and processes that do no violence to what is already established. But those writers who feel constricted by a mere solar system face a certain inconvenience when they set about taking their characters to the farther parts of our galaxy or to other galaxies. The fact is—and I apologize to all those for whom it is an odiously familiar fact—that to reach any but the nearest stars would take several hundred years even if one travelled at the speed of light, in the course of doing which one would, if I understand Einstein's popularisers correctly, become infinite in mass and zero in volume, and this is felt to be undesirable. A few writers simply accept this difficulty and arrange for their travellers to put themselves into some sort of deep-freeze until just before planetfall, or allow them to breed in captivity for the requisite number of generations, in which case the plot will concern what happens when a couple of centuries have elapsed and nobody on board is any longer aware of the situation. But most commonly, the author will fabricate a way of getting around Einstein, or even of sailing straight through him: a device known typically as the space-warp or the hyper-drive will make its appearance, though without any more ceremony than "He applied the space-warp," or "He threw the ship into hyper-drive." Such reticence may baffle and annoy the neophyte, as unfamiliar conventions will, but one would not demand that every Western include an exposition of ranching theory, and the space-warp is an equally acceptable convention, resting as it does on the notion that while there is a theoretical limit to the speed at which matter can be moved through space, there is no such limit to the speed at which space can be moved through space. Therefore, if the space being moved contains a space-ship, this can be shifted from the neighbourhood of the Earth to the neighbourhood of the Dog Star in an afternoon or so without any glaring affront to Einstein.

So much for real or good-imitation science; a few words now on the flagrantly pseudo variety. If aliens are to be introduced—alien is the term applied in the trade to any intelligent creature originating outside the Earth—the problem of communicating with them is likely to arise. Some excellent stories have been written about non-communicating aliens, from *The War of the Worlds* onwards, but their potentialities hardly extend beyond simple menace, and, as we shall see, recent science fiction has tended to lose interest in menace of this kind. Talking to an alien, however, presents difficulties that are literally insurmountable. One doesn't want to start too far back, but granted that communication, whatever it is, can be conceived of in other than human terms, and granted that it might involve something analogous to speech, one is still faced with a choice of infeasibilities. Direct learning of an alien language as one might under adverse conditions learn a human language, by ostensive definition and the like, entails presupposing an alien culture with human linguistic habits, which seems unlikely. The idea of a translation machine, recalling the space-warp in being usually introduced by phrases like "He set up the translation machine," differs from the space-warp in presenting a direct affront to common sense, for such a machine would clearly be foiled even by an utterance in Portuguese unless it had been "taught" Portuguese to start with. Telepathy—"The thought-forms of the alien flooded into his mind"—cannot exist. (Or can it? According to the director of its newly formed Astronautics Institute, the Westinghouse Electric Corporation is conducting research into telepathy as a means of long-distance communication.) My concern at the moment, however, is not that all these notions are, or may be, implausible, but that they are offered as plausible and that efforts are made to conceal their implausibility. The same is true of other traditional devices: time travel, for instance, is inconceivable, but if an apparatus of pseudo-logic is not actually set up to support it, the possibility of recourse to such an apparatus will not be explicitly ruled out. The science-fiction writer works by minimising what is self-contradictory.

Whether or not an individual story does justice to the laws of nature is a consideration that can affect our judgment of it, but my purpose here is to insist that such justice is always an aim—in the field of science fiction. The point of this is that immediately adjacent to this field, and in some instances to be distinguished from it only with difficulty, lies the field of fantasy. Fantasy of the kind I am going to discuss has developed into a self-contained form of writing in the same sense and over much the same period as science fiction: the two modes appeal to some of the same interests, share some of the same readership and unite in the name of a periodical, *The Magazine of Fantasy and Science Fiction*. It will be seen that I am using the term "fantasy" in a special and restricted sense, corresponding to a special kind of publication abutting upon my subject; I am aware of the existence of a body of work that can be called fantasy, from *Beowulf* to Kafka, which anticipates and parallels this kind of fantasy in a way that nothing quite anticipates or parallels science fiction, but my business is not with that. However, I acknowledge the fact that fantasy, in the special sense, gives, despite its much smaller volume, as valid a glimpse of contemporary attitudes as does science fiction. But I think it better to say straight out that I do not like fantasy, whether from *Beowulf* to Kafka, or in the specialised contemporary magazines, rather than take the trouble of devising reasons for my dislike, though I think I could do so if pressed. For now I merely intend to differentiate fantasy from science fiction, a task that involves little more than remarking that while science fiction, as I have been arguing, maintains a respect for fact or presumptive fact, fantasy makes a point of flouting these; for a furniture of robots, space-ships, techniques, and equations it substitutes elves, broomsticks, occult powers, and incantations. It may be to the purpose to quote an utterance by Fredric Brown, one of the most ingenious and inventive, though not one of the most self-questioning, writers of science fiction. In the introduction to his volume of short stories, *Star Shine*, we find Brown, who also writes fantasy on occasion, attempting to distinguish the two modes. After referring to the Midas myth—"remember it?" he asks, an apposite question when we try to imagine his readership, and goes on to give a summary—Brown says:

Let's translate that into science fiction. Mr. Midas, who runs a Greek restaurant in the Bronx, happens to save the life of an extraterrestrial from a far planet who is living in New York anonymously as an observer for the Galactic Federation, to which Earth for obvious reasons is not yet ready to be admitted. . . . The extraterrestrial, who is a master of sciences far beyond ours, makes a machine which alters the molecular vibrations of Mr. Midas's body so his touch will have a transmuting effect upon other objects. And so on. It's a science fiction story, or could be made to be one.

It might be thought that, to push it to the limit, a fantasy story could be turned into a science-fiction story merely by inserting a few lines of pseudo-scientific patter, and I would accept this as an extreme theoretical case, although I cannot think of an actual one. Even so, a difference which makes the difference between abandoning verisimilitude and trying to preserve it seems to me to make all the difference, and in practice the arbitrary and whimsical development of nearly every story of fantasy soon puts it beyond recovery by any talk of galactic federations or molecular vibrations. One parenthetical note: it should not be thought that no story dealing with elves and such can be science fiction. There are pixies and four-leafed clovers and cromlechs and the land of heart's desire in Eric Frank Russell's story "Rainbow's End," but these are mere apparatus in a sinister hypnotic attack on a band of interstellar explorers. Similarly, although vampirism is one of the staples of nineteenth-century fantasy, Richard Matheson's novel *I Am Legend* makes brilliantly ingenious and incidentally horrifying use of the myth for science-fiction purposes, whereby every traditional detail is explained along rational lines: the wooden stake through the heart, for instance, which put paid to Dracula and so many of his playmates, is necessary in order to maintain the distension of the wound—bullets and knives are no good for that job, and the microbe which causes vampirism is aerophobic.

While perhaps seeming to have kept our definition only distantly in view, I have in fact been rather deftly filling out and limiting its various implications. All that remains in this section is to describe a couple of codicils, kinds of narrative to be included on the grounds that they appeal to the same set of interests as science fiction in the sense defined, or at least are written and read by the same writers and readers. The first of these, numerically unimportant and readily disposed of, consists of stories about prehistoric man. Their existence can perhaps be blamed, for blame seems called for, on the fact that Wells wrote something called "A Story of the Stone Age"; I also note, though without at the moment doing more than note, that the subject reappears in *The Inheritors*, the second novel of the contemporary British writer William Golding, who comes nearer than anybody so far to being a serious author working within science fiction. But more of him later. The second supplementary category includes stories based on some change or disturbance or local anomaly in physical conditions. This accommodates several very familiar types of story, mostly involving novelties that threaten mankind. These may originate outside the Earth, as in Conan Doyle's "The Poison Belt" and Fred Hoyle's recent *The Black Cloud*, or on the Earth itself, as in John Christopher's *The Death of Grass*, published in the United States as *No Blade of Grass*. Alternatively, the author will chronicle some monstrous emergence arising from existing science and technology, especially, of course, the hydrogen bomb. The film industry has fallen gleefully upon that one, serving up a succession of beasts produced by mutation via radiation —giant ants, for instance, in *Them*—or else liberated from some primeval underground cavity by test explosions—

Rodan, a Japanese film, made great play with a brace of giant armour-plated radioactive supersonic pterodactyls finally despatched by guided missiles. Menaces of this kind naturally antedate the hydrogen bomb: an early and, I should guess, very influential example is Wells's unpleasantly vivid "The Empire of the Ants," in which the anomaly in question consists of an increase in intelligence, not in mere bulk. Although this is treated as having arisen in the course of evolution, not under artificial stimulus, the story has an obvious place in the development of its category. Finally, I should point out here, or hereabouts, that the last ten years have seen a perceptible decline in the role played in science fiction by actual science. The space-ship, for example, for a long time remained novel enough to be worth some description: nowadays it is often no more than a means of introducing characters into an alien environment, referred to as casually as an aeroplane or a taxi. Many stories of the future, again, and these commonly of the more interesting kind, take as their theme changes in the political or economic realm, with science and technology reduced to background detail: the hero will be served with Venusian flying-monkey steaks by a robot waiter, but the main business of his evening will be to persuade his fellow-members of the General Motors clan to take up the sword against the Chrysler clan. "*Science* fiction" is every day losing some of its appropriateness as a name for science fiction, and the kind of rearguard action that is being fought on its behalf by the commentators, on the plea that politics and economics and psychology and anthropology and even ethics are really or nearly as much sciences as atomic physics, is chiefly valuable as an indication of a state of mind. In any event, no alternative nomenclature so far suggested is applicable enough to justify the huge task of get-

ting it accepted in place of a term so firmly established as
the present one.

To restate matters, then: science fiction presents with
verisimilitude the human effects of spectacular changes in
our environment, changes either deliberately willed or in-
voluntarily suffered. I turn now to a brief and selective account of the ancestry of the form. To do so is at any rate
to follow an apparently unbreakable habit, except perhaps
as regards brevity, of those who discuss science fiction from
within the field. To be perpetually recounting its own history marks the attainment of a kind of puberty in the
growth of a mode or a style, and here we have yet another
parallel in development between science fiction and jazz.
The year 1441 is, I think, the earliest date to which anybody has yet traced back the origins of jazz; historians of
science fiction are likely to start off with Plato and the
Atlantis bits in the *Timaeus* and the *Critias*. From there
they will wander forward, usually lending their account
increased bulk and impressiveness by subsuming fantasy
as well as science fiction under the irritating heading of
"imaginative fiction," and taking in on the way the *Dia-
logues* of Pope Gregory I, the *Niebelungenlied* and *Beowulf*,
the Arthurian romances, Thomas More, Gulliver, *The Mys-
teries of Udolpho, Frankenstein*, a lot about Poe, *Dracula*,
Verne and Wells, arriving finally at the really climactic
event, the foundation of *Amazing Stories* in 1926. (All
these names, and very many more, are conscientiously dis-
cussed in L. Sprague de Camp's representative *Science Fiction Handbook*, published in 1953.) These manoeuvres,
which leave the jazz historian doing the best he can with
Ravel and Milhaud and what an honour it was for everybody when Stravinsky wrote the *Ebony Concerto* for Woody
Herman's band, perhaps recall the attempts of the Renaissance apologists to establish the respectability of poetry as

something neither obscene nor trivial, and there may be more than a merely verbal resemblance between the boast-fulness of much science-fiction propaganda and Scaliger's assertion that

Poetry represents things that are not, as if they were, and as they ought to be or might be. The poet makes another nature, hence he turns himself into another god: he also will create worlds.

Histories of science fiction, as opposed to "imaginative literature," usually begin, not with Plato or *The Birds* of Aristophanes or the *Odyssey*, but with a work of the late Greek prose romancer Lucian of Samosata. The distinction of this, the so-called *True History*, is that it includes the first account of an interplanetary voyage that the research-ers have managed to unearth, but it is hardly science fiction, since it deliberately piles extravagance upon extravagance for comic effect:

Relinquishing the pursuit, we set up two trophies, one for the infantry engagement on the spiders' webs, and one on the clouds for the air-battle. It was while we were thus engaged that our scouts announced the approach of the Cloud-centaurs, whom Phaethon had expected in time for the battle. They were indeed close upon us, and a strange sight, being compounded of winged horses and men; the human part, from the middle upwards, was as tall as the Colossus of Rhodes, and the equine the size of a large merchantman. Their number I cannot bring myself to write down, for fear of exciting incredulity.

It is no more than appropriate that Lucian's trip to the moon should be preceded by an encounter with some women who are grape-vines from the waist down and followed by sea-battles inside a whale's mouth, nor in particular that it should be accomplished by the travellers' ship being snatched up in a waterspout. Leaving aside the question whether there was enough science around in the second century to make science fiction feasible, I will merely remark that the sprightliness and sophistication of the *True History* make it read like a joke at the expense of nearly all early-modern science fiction, that written between, say, 1910 and 1940. I note finally Lucian's discovery that the men in the moon are of fantastic appearance and habits, but certainly not menacing in any way. The notion of nasty aliens is a comparatively recent one, although it is dominant in the early-modern period I have just defined. The contemporary alien tends to be not only not menacing, but so much better than man—morally rather than technologically—as to put him to shame. I am not quite sure what kind of deduction to draw from that graph, but there must be some.

It is not for a millennium and a half that, according to the canon, further attempts at a moon voyage appear. There might be thought to have been a good deal of science around in the 1630's, what with Kepler's work just finished, Galileo still doing his stuff, and astronomical observation improved to the point where for the first time the planet Mercury was observed in transit across the sun. However, Kepler's *Somnium*—published in 1634, the same year as the first English translation of Lucian's *True History*— evidently describes a trip to the moon in which demons are used as the power source, or rather the hero dreams that this is what is taking place. I find all this of compelling interest, but the plea of the science-fiction historians, that at that time you had little hope of getting to the moon except by dreaming about demons, fails to convince me that the *Somnium*, like the *True History*, is anything but fantasy. The same applies to Bishop Godwin's pro-Copernican romance, *Man in the Moone, or a Discourse of a Voyage Thither by Domingo Gonsales*, which was published in

1638, though probably written a good deal earlier, and was reprinted half a dozen times before the end of the century. Gonsales gets to the moon on a raft drawn by wild swans, a device which John Wilkins, chairman of the body which later became the Royal Society, considered to be quite sound in theory. The only point of much concern to us, however, is that the inhabitants of the moon are found to be what they regularly are in the earlier examples, creatures of a superior morality, any who fall far short of the required standard being infallibly detected and deported to Earth: "the ordinary vent for them," Godwin explains, "is a certain high hill in the North of America, whose people I can easily believe to be wholly descended of them."

I have given enough, I think, of the traditional roll call to establish its tendency, a heavy reliance on accidental similarities. This judgment certainly applies to the next book on everyone's list, Cyrano de Bergerac's *Voyage dans la Lune* (1650). After an abortive experiment with bottles of dew—the sun sucks up dew, you see—Cyrano gets to the moon in a chariot powered by rockets. It is much worse than pointless to take this as an "anticipation" of the engine recently fired at the moon by the Russians or of anything in recent literature, and the same is true of the fact that in Voltaire's *Micromégas* we have the first visit to Earth by an alien. One awaits the revelation that Spenser's Talus is the first, or at any rate an early, robot in English literature. A work more oddly omitted from science-fiction annals is *The Tempest*, in which the very features which must have caused it to be passed over—the comparatively factual outline, the approach by ship, instead of in a waterspout or by demon-propulsion—are the ones which should have brought it to notice. Furthermore, whatever *The Tempest* may be currently agreed to be about, I cannot help thinking that one of the things it is about is specialised knowledge, and whatever may be the relation currently devised between Jacobean science and magic, it would be safe to say that contemporary attitudes towards what we now see as two things were partly inseparable. Even if one resists the temptation to designate Caliban as an early mutant—"a freckled whelp," you remember, "not gifted with a human shape," but human in most other ways—and Ariel as an anthropomorphised mobile scanner, Prospero's attitude to them, and indeed his entire role as an adept, seems to some degree experimental as well as simply thaumaturgical. These considerations, I suggest, while not making the play anything but a very dilute and indirect influence on science fiction, do make it a distant anticipation. On a cruder level, the eccentric scientist-recluse and his beautiful daughter are an almost woefully familiar pair of stereotypes in all but the most recent science fiction, and, incidentally, large areas of what I might call the *Tempest* myth reappear in one of the best of the science-fiction films. The title was *Forbidden Planet*, which induces the reflection that planets have only in the last hundred years or less become the natural setting for this kind of writing; if we want to find early forms of it in days when the Earth was still incompletely explored and space was utterly inaccessible, the obvious place to look is not on other planets but in remote regions of our own, in particular, of course, undiscovered islands.

To mention *Gulliver's Travels* next is not likely to cause any surprise, nor, I hope, alarm. This work is clearly an ancestor of science fiction, and not on the grounds that Laputa is an early powered satellite, either. The claim rests firstly on the notorious pains taken by Swift to counterfeit versimilitude in the details of his story. Without attempting to draw an exact parallel, I submit that this is rather like the methods of science fiction, at any rate in that it serves

to dispel that air of arbitrariness, of having no further aim
than to be striking, which is characteristic of most fantasy:
the surprising behaviour of Lilliputian candidates for pre-
ferment would lose its effect, I take it, in an anti-realistic
context. All that businesslike thoroughness in description,
with everything given its dimensions, reappears noticeably
in the work of Jules Verne, where it constitutes the chief—
often the only—method of keeping the reader's disbelief
in some state of suspension. The other science-fiction thing
about *Gulliver's Travels* is that it presents, clearly enough,
a series of satirical utopias, these being chronicled with a
great power of inventing details that are to be consistent
with some basic assumption. This point, where invention
and social criticism meet, is the point of departure for a
great deal of contemporary science fiction, and no work is
more relevant than *Gulliver's Travels* to this part of our
investigation.

Some of these remarks apply to two other island utopias:
More's work and Bacon's *New Atlantis*. Of these, the Bacon
fragment more strongly recalls science fiction, in that some
of its marvels are technological, with research in meteor-
ology, medicine, horticulture, and methods of conjuring,
plus aeroplanes, submarines, and microtonal music using
echo-chambers. But neither *Utopia* nor *The New Atlantis*
match the intent and satirical preoccupation with the social
surface that we find both in the Swift and in, for instance,
Pohl and Kornbluth's *The Space Merchants*, from which I
quoted earlier. Both More and Bacon are, of course, dar-
lings of the science-fiction academics, together with many
another writer who falls short of grim documentary realism.
Typical omissions of more or less unexpectedness include
Chaucer, whose "Squire's Tale" surely includes an account
of an early flying machine, and the *Mundus Alter et Idem*
attributed to Bishop Hall (1607). The *Mundus*, tradition-

ally taken as a source of *Gulliver's Travels,* is a string of
comic-satiric utopias—the gluttons' paradise where stair-
cases are banned as difficult for eaters and dangerous for
drinkers, the feminist paradise where men do all the chores
and parliament is in perpetual session with everyone talking at once—that anticipates with weird precision another
Pohl and Kornbluth novel, *Search the Sky.* The Gothic
novel and its successors do get into the canon, but, with one
large exception, these, while all-important in the ancestry
of modern fantasy, scarcely prefigure science fiction. The
exception can hardly help being *Frankenstein,* which, albeit in a distorted form, has had a posthumous career of
unparalleled vigour; even old Dracula has less often been
exhumed in cinematic form and has never been mated or
allowed to re-galvanise himself. (I had better explain at
this point that the contemporary trade-term applying to the
monster is "android," a synthetic being roughly resembling
a man, as opposed to a robot, which is a mere peripatetic
machine.) The notable thing about Frankenstein the character is that, far from being possessed of supernatural
powers, he is a physiologist with academic training, a
feature he has retained in his modern incarnations, while
altogether losing the sentimental Shelleyan quality that
marked his original appearance. Frankenstein, in the popular mind, when not confused with his monster, is easily the
most outstanding representative of the generic mad scientist
who plagued bad early-modern science fiction and has now
been fined down* into the better-adjusted but still un-

* The career of the mad scientist flourishes unchecked in the modern
juvenile comic book. Those who see in this fact a conspiratorial attempt
to undermine public confidence in scientists (which would be a praiseworthy attempt anyhow, I should have thought) may be reassured to
find that these days the mad scientist tends to be deprived of his laboratory by other, saner scientists, rather than being overthrown by the two-
fisted space rangers. His Einstein haircut should be taken as a tribute
to the universality of that great figure.

sociable and eccentric scientist who, often with a Miranda-like daughter-secretary in attendance, continues to head an occasional research project and figure in the hero's thoughts as the Old Man. More important science-fiction themes than this, however, have radiated from the original book. It is true that, as L. Sprague de Camp observes, "all the shambling horde of modern robots and androids are descendants of Frankenstein's sadly malevolent monster," but beyond this lies the whole notion of the artificial creation which turns and rends its master. Čapek's *R.U.R.* (1920) was perhaps the first modern treatment of this notion, which still regularly reappears, a recent instance being Robert Sheckley's story "Watchbird." Here an airborne device, programmed to detect and forestall aggressive intentions, ends by prohibiting most kinds of human action. This idea generalises into innumerable fictionalised sermons on the dangers of overgrown technology which I shall be detailing later. Before leaving *Frankenstein*, it is worth observing that a third aspect of the scientific character descends from it, that of the morally irresponsible researcher indifferent to the damage he may cause or render possible, a kind of person consciously described by Wells in *The Island of Dr. Moreau*, where animals are vivisected in an attempt to humanise them, and to all appearance unconsciously in *The Food of the Gods*, where Herakleophorbia IV, the growth-inducing compound, is thrown on to the rubbish dump and swilled down the drains and generally scattered over the countryside in a fantastically light-hearted spirit. The irresponsible type of scientist is not altogether separable from a fourth type with a diverse ancestry, that to whom science is a route to personal power.

Some mention of Poe is sadly difficult to avoid in the present context: it has to be admitted that while he was much more important, perhaps to the point of being all-important, in the development of fantasy, he had in one sense a very direct influence on the development of science fiction. Before examining this, it may be just about worth while recalling that Poe seems to have invented the detective story, or so I remember being told at school. Without attempting to rival the complexity of my comparative analysis of jazz and science fiction, I should like to assert flatly that detective fiction and science fiction are akin. There is a closely similar exaltation of idea or plot over characterisation, and some modern science fiction, like most detective fiction, but unlike the thriller, invites the reader to solve a puzzle. It is no coincidence—how could it be?—that from Poe through Conan Doyle to Fredric Brown (the Midas expert) the writer of the one will often have some sort of concern with the other. Poe, at any rate, wrote a couple of stories involving balloon flight, at that time still a novelty, and another taking the destruction of the Earth as its point of departure. His unfinished novel, however, *The Narrative of A. Gordon Pym*, though sometimes cited, is a romance that wanders off into fantasy rather than having anything to do with science fiction. Such interest as it holds for us lies in the fact that Jules Verne's *An Antarctic Mystery* is a continuation, albeit an incoherent one, of the *Pym* narrative, and it is clear from innumerable resemblances, as well as from his own admission, that Verne learnt more from Poe than from any other writer.

With Verne we reach the first great progenitor of modern science fiction. In its literary aspect his work is, of course, of poor quality, a feature certainly reproduced with great fidelity by most of his successors. Although interspersed on occasion with fast and exciting narrative, for instance in the episode where Captain Nemo and his associates find their twenty-thousand-league voyage interrupted by the Antarctic ice pack, the story line is cluttered up again and again by long explanatory lectures and bald undramatised flashbacks. Even the more active passages are full of comically bad writing:

What a scene! The unhappy man, seized by the tentacle and fastened to its blowholes, was balanced in the air according to the caprice of this enormous trunk. He was choking, and cried out, "*A moi! à moi!*" (Help! help!). Those French words caused me a profound stupor. Then I had a countryman aboard, perhaps several! I shall hear that heartrending cry all my life!

The unfortunate man was lost. Who would rescue him from that powerful grasp? Captain Nemo threw himself on the poulp, and with his hatchet cut off another arm. His first officer was fighting with rage against other monsters that were climbing the sides of the *Nautilus*. The crew were fighting with hatchets.

The Canadian, Conseil, and I dug our arms into the fleshy masses. A violent smell of musk pervaded the atmosphere. It was horrible.

One would have to blame Verne's translator for some of those ineptitudes, but such was the form in which the novels reached English-speaking readers, none of whom, to my knowledge, has bothered to complain. The story and the ideas were the thing. These ideas, the scientific ones at least, have naturally got a bit dated: the helicopter with seventy-four horizontal screws, the tunnel to the centre of the Earth, the moon-ship shot out of a gun at a speed that would have pulped the travellers before they were clear of the barrel. But these errors hardly matter, any more than Swift's Brobdingnagians cease to be impressive when we reason that they would have broken most of their bones whenever they tried to stand up. It matters hardly more that Verne did successfully foretell the guided missile, nor that this extract from *Five Weeks in a Balloon* (1862) has a bearing on events of eighty years later:

"Besides," said Kennedy, "the time when industry gets a grip on everything and uses it to its own advantage may not be particularly amusing. If men go on inventing machinery they'll end by being swallowed up by their own inventions. I've often thought that the last day will be brought about by some colossal boiler heated to three thousand atmospheres blowing up the world."

"And I bet the Yankees will have a hand in it," said Joe.

The general prophecy about invention overreaching itself is clearly far more interesting than the particular glimpse of something like the nuclear bomb, or rather of its possible outcome. Verne's importance is that, while usually wrong or implausible or simply boring in detail, his themes foreshadow a great deal of contemporary thinking, both inside and outside science fiction.

As regards the mode itself, Verne developed the tradition of the technological utopia, presenting in *The Begum's Fortune* a rival pair of these, the one enlightened and paternalistic, the other totalitarian and warlike. This was published in 1879, so it is no surprise to find that the nice utopia is French and the nasty one German. There are also several novels virtually initiating what has become a basic category of science fiction, the satire that is also a warning, and it is here that Verne is of some general interest. Thus in *Round the Moon*, after the projectile has fallen back into the sea—at a speed of 115,200 miles an hour, incidentally, and without hurting anyone inside—we find a company being founded to "develop" the moon after a fashion that anticipates *The Space Merchants*. The sequel to *Round the Moon, The Purchase of the North Pole*, involves not only the said purchase on the part of the Baltimore Gun Club, the people who set up the cannon to fire the moon-projectile, but a scheme whereby a monstrous explosion shall alter the inclination of the Earth's axis and so bring the polar region into the temperate zone. Since parts of the civilised world would correspondingly be shifted into new polar regions, the response of officialdom is unfavourable. However, the explosion takes place, and only an error in the calculations preserves the *status quo*. The notion of an advancing technology increasing the destructive power of unscrupulousness reappears on a smaller scale in *The Floating Island*, where the huge artifact breaks up in mid-ocean as a result of rivalry between two financial cliques. The book closes with a straightforward Vernean sermon on the dangers of scientific progress considered as an embodiment of human arrogance. The heavy moral tone of this and many passages in the other books is among the less fortunate of Verne's legacies to modern science fiction, and some of his other anticipations, if they are properly that, give no cause for congratulation. In particular, his sexual interest is very thin: Phileas Fogg, the hero of *Around the World in Eighty Days*, does pick up an Indian princess in the course of his travels, but we discover almost nothing about her, and Fogg treats her with an inflexible courtesy which goes beyond mere Victorianism and which any girl of spirit might find subtly unflattering. Even the villains rarely do so much as aspire to lechery. It is in his political tone, which, however vague and eccentric, is nearly always progressive, and even more in his attitude to technology, fascinated but sceptical and at times tinged with pessimism, that Verne's heritage is most interesting and valuable: his last book, *The Eternal Adam*, is a kind of proleptic elegy for the collapse of Western civilisation. These are the considerations which go some way to override his ineptitude and pomposity, his nineteenth-century boys'-story stuffiness, and make him, not only in a science-fiction sense, recognisably modern.

Whatever else he may or may not have been, Jules Verne

is certainly to be regarded as one of the two creators[*] of modern science fiction; the other, inevitably enough, is H. G. Wells. To treat Wells as such, rather than as the first important practitioner in an existing mode, is no denigration. Rather, it takes account of the fact that all his best and most influential stories appeared between 1895 and 1907, before science fiction had separated itself from the main stream of literature, and so were written, published, reviewed, and read as "romances" or even adventure stories. The expected comparison with Verne, made often enough at the time (though repudiated by both), now shows not only a huge disparity in literary merit but certain differences in the direction of interest. A main preoccupation of Verne's, as I said, was technology itself, "actual possibilities," as Wells put it, "of invention and discovery," and this holds true equally when what were possibilities to Verne are impossibilities or grotesque improbabilities to us. The long scientific lectures interpolated in his stories—"If I created a temperature of 18°, the hydrogen in the balloon will increase by 18/480s, or 1,614 cubic feet" and so on— these lectures, however tedious, are highly germane to what Verne was doing. Wells, on the other hand, is nearly always concerned only to fire off a few phrases of pseudo-scientific patter and bundle his characters away to the moon or the

[*] There were, of course, innumerable other ancestors of secondary importance. The volume of utopian literature in the second half of the nineteenth century is huge, and its range stretches all the way from tract-like, plotless dogmatisms of politics, economics, or religion to adventure stories with a few ideas in them. Some of these works were of great and prolonged popularity: the classic instance is Edward Bellamy's *Looking Backward*, with its world-wide sale and its dozens of rejoinders. The vogue of this kind of writing was such that Gilbert and Sullivan, who had a sharp eye for fashions in taste if for nothing else, thought it worth a whole operetta, *Utopia Ltd.* (first performed in 1893), which I have so far been unable to see performed. Nor was this an interest confined to specialists or cranks, as is testified by the existence of utopian works by Bulwer Lytton, Samuel Butler, W. H. Hudson, William Morris, and William Dean Howells.

803rd century with despatch. Verne himself saw this point all right, and complained after reading (rather cursorily, it seems) *The First Men in the Moon*:

I make use of physics. He fabricates. I go to the moon in a cannon-ball discharged from a gun. There is no fabrication here. He goes to Mars [*sic*] in an airship [*sic*], which he constructs of a metal that does away with the law of gravitation. That's all very fine, but show me this metal. Let him produce it.

It is often said that Wells's main interest was not in scientific advance as such but in its effect on human life. Although this is true of some of his works, as we shall see in a moment, it is patently not true of the ones which had the most immediate effect on the growth of science fiction. Indeed, in this respect the Verne of *The Floating Island* or *The Purchase of the North Pole* seems distinctly more contemporary than the Wells of *The Time Machine* or *The Invisible Man*. The real importance of these stories is that they liberated the medium from dependence on extrapolation and in so doing initiated some of its basic categories. The time machine itself, the Martians and their strange irresistible weapons in *The War of the Worlds*, the monsters in the first half of *The Food of the Gods*, the other world coterminous with ours in "The Plattner Story," the carnivorous plant in "The Flowering of the Strange Orchid," all these have had an innumerable progeny. What is noticeable about them is that they are used to arouse wonder, terror, and excitement, rather than for any allegorical or satirical end. When the Time Traveller finds that mankind will have become separated into two races, the gentle ineffectual Eloi and the savage Morlocks, the idea that these are descended respectively from our own leisured classes and manual workers comes as a mere explanation, a solution to the puzzle; it is not transformed, as it inevitably would be in a modern writer, into a warning about some current trend in society. *The Invisible Man* is only very incidentally concerned with the notion that a scientific discovery may be dangerously two-edged; the novel is about the problems, firstly of being, secondly of catching, an invisible man. "The Country of the Blind," which is science fiction of the physical-change variety, is about what it would be like for a sighted person in a country of the blind: the proverb about the one-eyed man being king there doubtless inspired the story, but its theme is a concretisation, not a daring imaginative statement, of the untruthful aspect of that proverb. A contemporary writer, again, would have used the proposed blinding of the hero as a climactic point for the enfilading of our intolerance towards exceptional talents; Wells throws this away in an aside, giving us the hero of an adventure story in danger, not the representative of anything being threatened with anything representative. Dr. Moreau's beast-men are beast-men, not symbolic puppets enacting a view of beasts and men, or of men. *The First Men in the Moon* admittedly has some satirical discussions of war and human irrationality, together with one of several early anticipations of the conditioning-during-sleep idea Huxley developed in *Brave New World*, but Wells's main drive here is simple delight in invention, in working out an alien ecology, typical of what I might call primitive science fiction.

Despite the fluent imaginativeness of the stories mentioned, the most forceful of Wells's romances is the strongly Verne-like *The War in the Air* of 1907. This curious synthesis of World Wars I, II, and III, with Germany attacking the United States before both are overwhelmed by a Chinese-Japanese coalition, is certainly concerned with the effect of technology on mankind, since the one is made to reduce the other to barbarism, and being both

satire and warning, it has, in the science-fiction context at
any rate, an unmistakably modern ring. *The War in the
Air*, however, rates comparatively little attention from the
commentators, as do Wells's utopian romances and their
not-so-remote ancestor of the early Fabian period, William
Morris's *News From Nowhere. Men Like Gods*, with its
nudism, or *In the Days of the Comet*, where a strange gas
so fills humanity with loving-kindness that everyone gets
started on companionate marriage, have none of the fire
of the early Wells, and give a soporific whiff of left-wing
crankiness, but their virtual exclusion from the modern
science-fiction canon is surprising. This part of Wells's output anticipated, but evidently did not influence, later developments. Even "A Story of the Days to Come," an early
and lively piece, never gets a mention, and yet it forecasts
the modern satirical utopia with fantastic exactness: advertising matter is everywhere bawled out of loudspeakers,
phonographs have replaced books, mankind is urbanized to
the point where agriculturalists commute in reverse, huge
trusts reign supreme, an army of unemployables is maintained by a kind of international poorhouse called the
Labour Company, all children are brought up in State
crèches, deviates get their antisocial traits removed by hyp-
nosis, dreams can be obtained to order, and as a last detail,
a prophecy so universal nowadays as to justify panic in
razor-blade circles, men don't shave any more, they use
depilatories. Quite likely Wells will soon get all, instead of
part, of the recognition as pioneer he clearly deserves.

The next part of the story, covering the early years of modern science fiction, depends for documentation upon sources difficult of access, for there cannot be many files of forty-year-old magazines outside private hands. The canon at this point tends to resemble those name-dropping catalogues, part acknowledgements, part bibliography, that I seem to remember coming up with some frequency in works of Middle English Literature. However, in April, 1911, a story called "Ralph 124C 41+: a romance of the year 2660" began to appear serially in a magazine called *Modern Electrics*. The author, a certain Hugo Gernsback, was also founder-editor of the magazine. Gernsback occupies a position in science fiction analogous to that of George Lewis in jazz, or perhaps, to be scholarly, that of Jelly Roll Morton, who likewise is no more than a name to most people, though Gernsback's has been commemorated in the name of the Oscar of the science-fiction world, the trophy known as the Hugo. At any rate, "Ralph 124C 41+" concerns the technological marvels invented or demonstrated by the ridiculously resourceful eponymous hero, whose plus-sign represents membership of a sort of scientific Order of Merit, and who starts off by burning up from three thousand miles away an avalanche that threatens the heroine in her native Switzerland. After some trouble with a pair of rival suitors, one human, the other Martian, Ralph restores the dead girl to life by a complicated deep-freeze and blood-transfusion technique. Other wonders include the hypnobioscope, a second anticipation of Huxley's hypnopaedia, and three-dimensional colour television, a term which Gernsback is credited, if that is the word, with having invented. Various successors to "Ralph 124" & so on began to appear, chiefly in magazines supposedly devoted to popular-science articles, but it was not until 1926 that Gernsback was able to found the first journal exclusively dedicated to science fiction, *Amazing Stories*, which is still with us. At this time and for some years afterwards, science fiction continued to be overshadowed, as regards bulk and circulation, by work in two adjacent fields.

The more important of these is fantasy, which I tried to differentiate in the previous section. *Weird Tales*, the first magazine of modern fantasy, was founded three years earlier than *Amazing Stories*, and I need do no more than allude to the existence—somewhere in the background—of Algernon Blackwood, Lord Dunsany, and Cabell's *Jurgen*. The most representative writer of the *Weird Tales* school was H. P. Lovecraft, much of whose work is horror fiction of the kind popular in England, at any rate, in the '20's and '30's. Some of Lovecraft's stories, "The Dunwich Horror," for instance, achieve a memorable nastiness; one or two, like "The Rats in the Walls," cross the boundary into the field of the ghost story, or are so anthologised, and a piece called "The Colour out of Space" occasionally finds its way into science-fiction collections, chiefly I imagine on account of its title. Lovecraft's intrinsic importance is small, but he does give that impression of being much more than ripe for psychoanalysis which pervades much fantasy and early science fiction, and the difficulty of categorising some of his work faithfully reflects the confusion of a period when non-realistic writing was in the throes of internal fission.

The other adjacent field competing with science fiction is conveniently described as space-opera, justly recalling the horse-opera which, under a skin of molecular thinness, it so much resembles. In space-opera, Mars takes the place of Arizona with a few physical alterations, the hero totes a blaster instead of a six-gun, bad men are replaced by bad aliens looking just like bad men with green skins and perhaps a perfunctory sixth digit, and Indians turn up in the revised form of what are technically known as bug-eyed monsters, a phrase often abbreviated to BEMs under the psychobiological law that terms frequently used will undergo shortening. Some commentators are opposed to the BEM, and adopt a characteristic self-righteousness in rapping poor Wells over the knuckles for having started the fashion with his Martians. This attitude seems justified if the BEM is a mere surrealist orangutan, rushing off into the Venusian swamp with the heroine in his tentacles, but menace is in itself a legitimate effect, and I have read many a good BEM story. A. E. van Vogt's *Voyage of the Space Beagle*, for instance, moves well for sixty thousand words simply by introducing a succession of BEMs, each nastier than the one before.

Actually, BEMs are not a *sine qua non* of space-opera, and early examples often fill up with stuff lifted from the historical novel, or if you like the parry-and-thrust opera, things like princesses and palace guards and ancient codes of honour. Later space-opera fills up from the 'tec yarn, with galactic hoodlums, alien dope-runners, etc. The kind of setup I have been describing is plainly an important ancestor and collateral of much contemporary fare as seen in comic books and strips aimed at those of immature age or inclination, and it even afflicts the occasional story in the serious science-fiction magazines. Moreover, space-opera with a full complement of BEMs and a small staff of mad scientists attended by scantily clad daughters constitutes, I should guess, the main brand-image of science fiction in the minds of the less *au-courant* trend-hounds, those who haven't yet caught on to how frightfully significant it all is. To go back in the other direction: the ancestral figure in the development of space-opera is clearly Rider Haggard, who in a book like *She* provided elements that needed only to be shifted to Mars and eked out with a BEM or two to get the whole new show on the road. Edgar Rice Burroughs performed this very feat in 1912 with *Under the Moons of Mars*, later republished as *A Princess of Mars*, and in the next quarter of a century or so more than a dozen successors flowed from his dreadfully fluent pen. The degree of scientific interest here can be gauged from the way Burroughs shows his contempt for all interplanetary devices, from watersprouts to gravity insulators: the hero, trapped in a cave by a band of Apaches, simply finds himself on Mars, and at once enough starts happening in the way of green men for the more technical questions to be quietly dropped. Burroughs' most celebrated and profitable creation, Tarzan, is, incidentally, a more complicated person than the continuing spate of films about him would suggest. Far from being a mere rescuer of lost wayfarers and converser with animals, he meets several adventures stemming even more directly from Rider Haggard, *Tarzan and the Lost Empire* or *Tarzan and the City of Gold*, for instance, which represent a kind of terrestrial space-opera,* and at least once, in *Tarzan at the Earth's*

* This is not a totally unfair label for a whole mode of writing located somewhere on the borders of science fiction: the tale of the lost race or undiscovered human tribe. Although most of the less accessible parts of the world have been ransacked to provide habitation for these isolates—from Atlantis and Mu to Tibet and the Grand Canyon, from

Core, we retrace the steps of Verne, though with a less dig-
nified gait.

During the 1930's, science fiction established itself,
separating with a slowly increasing decisiveness from fantasy and space-opera, advancing in bulk and popularity
(most of the time there were at least half a dozen pulps
running), but remaining firmly at a humble level of literary
endeavour. Some stories leaned heavily on the scientific
element, echoing Verne in their reliance on technology, or
gadgetry, occasionally far outdoing him both in degree of
theoretical complication and in unreadability. For the most
part, however, vulgarisations of the early Wells held the
field, setting up a pseudo-scientific base for a tale of wonder
and terror. I can remember one that fused Lucian with
"The Flowering of the Strange Orchid," featuring a plant
growth whose upper half was the upper half of a large and
fierce young lady. Another introduced a disguised alien
leading a supposed mineralogical expedition to a remote
underground chamber, where his friends awaited a hasty
breakfast of human flesh before setting off to conquer the
world. Although disposing of much lethal machinery, they
never got their breakfast and expired in a shower of sparks.
(I seem to recall that that one was rather well written,
though I was only about twelve at the time.) Then there
was the one about the scientist, not actually mad, but
sternly denounced by his colleagues as irresponsible, who
created life in the laboratory. The life was a sort of rubbery
jellyfish that engulfed things, not at all unlike the Blob

---

the polar regions to the bowels of the earth—it is rare to find anything
beyond an "adventure" interest emerging. Lord Lytton's *The Coming
Race* (1891) and Joseph O'Neill's *Land Under England* (1935), which
occur somewhere near the beginning and end of the period in which the
theme was popular, are relatively isolated examples of its use for didactic
and admonitory purposes—purposes recognisably characteristic of serious
science fiction.

recently on view at our theatres—it was soon frozen into submission with dry-ice extinguishers. This early version was far tougher and at one stage successfully engulfed H.M.S. *Invincible*, on manoeuvres at the time in the North Atlantic. Finally, during its traditional task of attacking Manhattan Island, its creator managed to destroy it at the price of personal engulfment. As far as I know none of these pieces has ever been reprinted, but those of the same period which have show a similar lack of subtlety and an almost incredible ignorance of, or indifference to, elementary literary pitfalls. Here is an extract from a story called "The Monster from Nowhere," published in 1935. One of the characters is telling his friends about an unpleasant experience on the Maratan Plateau:

"We all looked then. And we saw . . . huge, amorphous blobs of jet black, which seemed to be of the earth, yet not quite of it. Sometimes these ever-changing fragments were suspended in air, with no visible support. At other times they seemed to rest naturally enough on solid ground. But ever and ever again—they changed!

"Afire with curiousity, we went to the open spot. It was a mistake."

"A mistake?" I said.

"Yes. Fletcher lost his life—killed by his own curiosity. I need not tell you how he died. It was, you must believe me, horrible. Out of nowhere, one of the jet blobs appeared before him . . . then around him . . . then—he was gone!"

"Gone!" exclaimed Ki. "You mean—dead?"

"I mean gone! One second he was there. The next, both he and the *thing* which had snatched him had disappeared into thin air.

"Toland and I fled, panic-stricken, back to camp. We told Gainelle what we had seen. Gainelle, a crack shot and a gallant sportsman, was incredulous; perhaps even dubious. . . ."

But whichever he was it did him no good, I'm afraid; a *thing* gets him as well. The point about this story, however (and there are plenty of others which prolong their flights of ineptitude nearly as far), is that it is not just a matter of *things*: their origin and the reason for their strange habits are explained quite conscientiously, though in the same repulsive style. "The Monster from Nowhere" is a good instance of the interesting idea badly set out, a very common phenomenon in science fiction even today, and I might remark here that nothing differentiates the addict from the inquirer more than the readiness of the former, and the understandable reluctance of the latter, to finish a story of this kind. Even I myself feel I should have read a little more really unreadable stuff in preparation for this investigation.

The present era in science fiction opened quite suddenly round about 1940; there were five magazines in 1938, thirteen in 1939, and twenty-two in 1941. (These of course were American; Britain had two publications of this sort at the time.) This expansion of outlet virtually coincided with the arrival of a large group of new writers in the field, among them many of the best-known names of today. Sensationalism began to diminish, some degree of literacy made its appearance, and the admonitory utopia, virtually the leading form of contemporary science fiction, came into being again after something like twenty years. The mode had not come of age—it has yet to do that—but at least its crawling days were over. Why this happened when it did, or at all, I am not sure. I cannot feel, for example, that World War II had much to do with it. The sudden increase in the number of magazines can perhaps be explained in part by the tendency of people who dislike the thought or the actuality of military service to grab at a gaudily covered pulp on a newsstand, but the stuff inside would be too full of conflict and unpleasantly possible weapons of war, I should have thought, to provide much of an escape: the funnies, true-life romances, or straight pornography would surely be better. As regards the emergence of the new and better writers, I can just suggest that while in 1930 you were quite likely to be a crank or a hack if you wrote science fiction, by 1940 you could be a normal young man with a career to start, you were a member of the first generation who had grown up with the medium already in existence. More simply, few things are much good to begin with, and the inferiority of early Elizabethan drama is not what makes Shakespeare's appearance remarkable.

Contemporary science fiction has not, I need hardly say, finally and everywhere turned its back on BEMs or stylistic imbecility. Let me tell you about a short work called "Legacy of Terror" in the November, 1958, issue of *Amazing Stories*. Holly Kendall, a six-foot-tall siren in "abbreviated shorts and light cotton sweater," is driving through the Vermont wastes on her way to tidy up at the experimental laboratory of her recently deceased father, in life a "tall, gentle man" with "soft voice and distant eyes." Encountering en route an ant as tall as herself, Holly retreats in panic, more or less into the arms of a young man:

He wasn't handsome, but you couldn't help being attracted to his wide, boyish grin, or being respectful to the steady, penetrating gaze of his deep brown eyes. He was tanned, and the grin he gave her flashed white against his skin.

"I do believe you," he said. "My name's Bryce Cooper; I've been looking for these big bugs for the past month. This is about as close as I came."

"You—you're looking for them?"

"That's right. I'm an associate professor at the university; English Lit's my racket, but I got me a degree in entymology, too. So when I picked up reports of king-sized spiders and stuff in the vicinity . . ." etc.

Very little later in the same scene, Bryce proposes marriage to Holly, mentioning that he earns $5,120 a year. Access to her father's journal leads Holly to the conclusion that the old man had been working on how to get souls to trans-migrate during life, that the ant had got to its present size through having the soul of a horse or something injected into it, and that Bryce, alongside his increasingly amorous behaviour, is actually her own father making free with Bryce's body. An "unholy glitter" rapidly comes into the eyes of the composite male ("Mad? An interesting conclu-sion, Hollyhocks"), he decides to kill the girl to ensure her silence and is stung to death in the nick of time by the king-sized bumblebee. Finally, when Holly tries to burn her father's journal, the parish priest prevents her, explain-ing "gently" that the professor's work must be carried on, for all understanding leads to God.

From this wealth of analysable material—only the detail about entymology perhaps banishes the suspicion that some fearsome cynic is responsible—very little needs to be singled out, not even the incest motif, the obtrusion of which bears witness rather to the author's naïveté, I feel, than to any-thing sinister in him or his readers or our culture. Before leaving this bumper number of *Amazing Stories*,* I will

---

* Its cover would delight any cultural diagnostician of pretension with its triad of horror (the king-sized ant, here blown up to emperor size), greed (Holly's Cadillac), and lust (Holly). The cover of a recent num-ber of *Super-Science Fiction* simplifies matters further by depicting a space-girl, even more generously shaped than Holly, on the point of en-gulfment by a tentacled Thing, an event uncommemorated in any of the stories inside. In fairness to *Amazing Stories*, I might add here that it is a model of refinement compared with some of the stuff in this "Third Monster Issue!" of *Super-Science Fiction*. Passing over "Mon-sters That Once Were Men" and "Birth of a Monster," I draw attention to "The Horror in the Attic"—"it was a hideous, horrible THING on a

just mention that it also contains a story called "Mission: Murder!," of which the moral is that terrorism and summary execution are justified if the enemy is dangerous and unpleasant enough—evidence of a political attitude notably rare in contemporary science fiction. The same issue carries a new adventure of Johnny Mayhem, a slightly less incredible version of Superman, and a sensible, vigorously written, apparently well-informed article attacking some of the policies of the Atomic Energy Commission.

This co-presence of the adult with the stupidly or nastily adolescent is highly characteristic of the modern science-fiction magazines, of which we might now make a general inspection. Their number and circulation continues to fluctuate with surprising sharpness—there was a notable drop, I am told, immediately after the launching of the first Russian sputnik—but the present tendency* is clearly one of expansion, with twenty or more titles coming out monthly or, occasionally, bi-monthly. In the current year we can expect something between one hundred and fifty and two hundred complete novels and collections of short stories, of which only about half will be paperbacks. A tendency for

---

gruesome errand." The errand consists of frightening to death the lover of a fifteen-year-old girl and then of eating the girl alive:

The creature held her tightly. With one massive paw it ripped away her clothing, tossing the tattered garments to the floor, exposing her firm white breasts, her soft woman's body. Close up, she could see the creature's teeth—hideous yellow fangs, [etc. etc.].

Before giving way to panic at such a cultural manifestation, one would do well to remember that vampires, werewolves, and such were behaving exactly like that over a hundred years ago, fulfilling the same function of putting into acceptable form interests that realistic fiction could not accommodate: Sheridan Le Fanu's "Carmilla," with its blatantly lesbian theme, is the most famous example.

* Since this was written there has been another drop, viewed in the relevant circles with wonderfully spontaneous concern. Voluble anxiety about its own commercial future has always been a demerit of the science-fiction industry, one which may be expected to disappear if the medium attains respectability.

established publishers to open a science-fiction list can also be detected, and there are two paperback houses turning out nothing else. It seems that, despite regular jeremiads from editors and authors, the medium is not yet in disrepair. If I now go on to concentrate for a moment on the magazines, it is because they afford a far more catholic view of the field, and far more clues to the nature of its readership, than do anthologies or individual volumes. These, in any case, regularly derive something like sixty per cent of their material from the magazines. The physical aspect of the latter is uniformly repellent, far more so than could be excused by any talk of the technical exigencies of pulp publication. Crude sensationalism vies with crude whimsy on the covers, and although wit occasionally makes an appearance—a recent one had a pirate boarding a spacecraft with a slide rule between his teeth—many a potential recruit to the medium must have been lost without having to stretch out a hand. It is hard to believe that anything likely to interest a grown man could lie under a cover-picture of a multi-armed alien Santa Claus, or within a journal called *Fantastic Universe* or *Astounding Science Fiction*, but I hope to establish that these natural suspicions are often unjustified. They would not be much lulled, admittedly, by a quick look through the interior of any given issue, which offers advertisements of the Rosicrucians and of Royal Jelly ("it's the secret of prolonged life"), of firms offering computer construction kits—125 computers with Geniac, only $19.95, or 150 small ones with Brainiac for only $17.95*; more appalling art-work; and silly editorial

---

* The cheaper and nastier magazines offer material that is more sinister (or more absurd). Here, though presumably not only here, you are given the chance of mail-ordering for $1.00 the Exploding Army Hand Grenade (Exact Replica):

Here's real battle authenticity. This menacing hand grenade looks and works just like a real one. All you do is pull the pin, wait 4 seconds,

epigraphs: "Hunted by the living and haunted by the dead
. . . Blaine had to do a lot better than merely look alive
to stay alive in this grim world!"—this prefixed to an ex-
ceptionally able and original story. If the stage of actually
beginning to read is attained, the material will be found
to include a novella of perhaps fifteen thousand words,
three or four short stories of between three and eight thousand words each, sometimes an instalment of a three- or
four-part serial running up to fifteen thousand (failing that,
another novella or a couple of shorts), editorial matter often
marked by a hectoring, opinionated tone, readers' letters
covering a staggering range of IQs, a book-review section
conducted with intelligence and a much greater readiness
to be nasty than one finds, say, in the Sunday *Times*, in
some cases a popular-science article on atomic physics, sea
serpents, telepathy, or the evaporation of the Caspian Sea,
and an interesting department in which are tabulated the
results of the readers' voting on the stories in the previous
issue—these are arranged in order of popularity and, in at
least one case, the author receiving the most votes regularly
gets a cash bonus from the publisher. While there is a lot

---

*throw the grenade, and watch the fun as it explodes automatically. It's
completely harmless, but the explosion it makes can be heard for a
block. Really scatters the gang when you throw this baby in their midst.
It sure looks and sounds real,* [etc. etc.].

If your interests differ slightly, what about a "Stuffed" Girl's Head for
only $2.98?

*Blondes, redheads and brunettes for every man to boast of his con-
quests . . . the first realistic likeness of the exciting women who play
an important part in every man's life . . . and one of the nicest qualities
is that they don't talk back! Accurately modelled to three-quarters life-
size and molded of skin-textured pliable plastic, these heads are so
life-like they almost breathe. Saucy, glittering eyes, full sensuous mouth
and liquid satin complexion, combined with radiant hair colors give
astonishing realism to these rare and unique Trophies. Blonds* [sic],
*redhead or brunette mounted on a genuine mahogany plaque is complete
and ready to hang on the wall for excitement and conversation.*

of reason for calling the devotees of science fiction uncritical, there is no doubt that in what must often be an ill-instructed way they are far more concerned about the merit of the stories they read than, for instance, the people who buy women's magazines. I shall return to this point in a moment.

To offer a full-dress division of contemporary science fiction into thematic categories would be laborious and out of proportion to its critical usefulness; here instead is a brief gallop through the fiction contents of a representative recent magazine. The October, 1958, *Astounding Science Fiction*, then, kicks off with a story by Clifford D. Simak, who has been writing the stuff for twenty-five years. In the present instance, a small country trader discovers a short-cut from his house into another world and sets up a bartering arrangement with its inhabitants. The main cruxes are (a) that the arrangement will not work without the intervention of the trader's dull-witted and despised neighbour, who turns out to be telepathic; and (b) that out of sympathy for the neighbour, and feeling that his own house ought to remain his, the trader insists that no outsiders, from the local Chamber of Commerce to the United Nations, shall be allowed to interfere. Thus the rights of the individual are—perhaps rather dully—upheld against the forces of convention and authority. The next story, "The Yellow Pill," by another established writer, presumptively introduces a psychiatrist in New York trying to cure a patient of the delusion that both of them are actually aboard a space-ship in flight. After some exchanges, in which each party systematically explains the other's world in terms of his own, the supposed psychiatrist swallows the yellow pill, an anti-delusion compound which works by amplifying sense-data, and finds himself on board a space-ship. Meanwhile, the other man has acquired the psychiatrical delusion, imagines himself cured of the space-ship delusion, and walks out of the door, which unfortunately leads into empty space instead of the outer office. This is mainly an ingenious little puzzle-thriller, but it also grapples—perhaps rather dully—with an aspect of solipsism. "Big Sword," by a newer author, shows us a distant planet harbouring an intelligent telepathic race of minute size but with some powers of self-defence. When the human expedition is about to destroy a colony of these creatures, out of inadvertence rather than malice, it is left to a small boy to strike up communication with the aliens and persuade his elders to offer them assistance instead of casual harm. Outwardly, the story falls into a familiar category, the biological puzzle (the aliens have a partly vegetable life-cycle that defeats understanding for some time), but again something is clearly being said—not so dully this time—about the rights of the insignificant and the outlandish. There is some sexual interest here, but minor and highly respectable. There is some too in the next story, ". . . And Check the Oil," even more minor and hardly less respectable; the rest of it is an inconclusive but not illiterate space-filler about some amiable visiting aliens who run out of food. Finally, "False Image" shows alien and man agreeing to overlook the differences of appearance and habit that repel or frighten each of them and so coming to an understanding.

You will have to take my word for it that none of these five stories is offensive in style, since extracts demonstrating inoffensiveness make for wearisome reading. Anyway, there are no degrees in entymology or wide, boyish grins here. Nor, you will have noticed, are there any king-sized spiders or BEMs of any sort. All four of the alien races introduced are friendly creatures, raising difficulties in communication only. In three out of five cases—a representative proportion, probably—there is recognisable moral concern of a sort: I am not interested for the moment in just what sort, merely in noting its presence. I could, of course, go on to note other shared characteristics, such as the comparatively minor role played by science, pseudo-science, technology, gadgetry, sex, but I think I have said enough about the October *Astounding* and the November *Amazing* to have evoked the experience of reading a science-fiction magazine in all its multifariousness and majesty. I have only to add the practical tip that, in addition to *Astounding*, the other periodicals of pretension are *Galaxy Science Fiction* and *The Magazine of Fantasy and Science Fiction*, before rounding off this section with a brief note on other outlets.

Anthologies of short stories, virtually all reprinted from magazines, form a strikingly high proportion, something like a quarter, of total publication in volume form, another quarter being formed by individual collections of shorts or novellas, most of which will also have appeared earlier in magazines. Of the remaining half, the novels, a large minority will be originals, but probably the bulk can again be traced back to the magazines, either in serial or in rudimentary form. It will be seen firstly that science fiction is to a great extent a short-story form, another point for later consideration, secondly that the magazines are a decisive source. A third deduction might be that people like reading stories twice over, or are unaware of doing so, but in fact the number of magazines makes it impossible to catch more than a few of the good stories as they come out, unless one is doing so full-time. A footnote on distribution is that science-fiction stories are spreading into general magazines, including *Playboy*, *Harper's*, *Esquire*, *McCall's*, *Good Housekeeping*, the *Reporter*, and the *Saturday Evening Post*. Science fiction has also appeared in *Ellery Queen's Mystery Magazine*, *Cats*, and *PEN* (The Public Employees' News).

A survey of readership can start with a figure or two: *Galaxy* sells about 125,000 an issue in the United States, plus editions in England, France, Belgium, Switzerland, Germany, Italy, Finland, and Sweden, in the appropriate languages. The Swedes are reported to be particularly keen, which recalls the fact that they are also the most jazz-conscious nation in Europe. *Astounding* has its foreign editions and sells something like 100,000 an issue in America, 35,000 in England, with subscribers in Africa, the Near East, Russia, and China. *Amazing*, which seems to circulate only in English, has an American sale of 50,000. Taking into account the tendency whereby those who read science fiction at all will read *Astounding*, and presupposing a good deal of swapping between enthusiasts, one comes up with a total science-fiction readership in the United States of something approaching half a million. Numbering about three-tenths of one per cent of the population, this is far from being a mass audience, a conclusion supported by the qualities of the material. Without making extravagant claims, one can suggest that the characteristics attributable to a mass medium—expensiveness, avoidance of the obscure or heterodox, reassuringness, anonymity—do not appear in a considerable quantity of contemporary science fiction, and I remind you that *Galaxy*, which rarely utilises BEMs or salacity, sells two and a half times as well as *Amazing*, in which they appear less rarely. I might just momentarily expand the point about anonymity by asserting that the best-known science-fiction writers are the reverse of anonymous or interchangeable: they are more likely to be annoyingly idiosyncratic. Moreover, readers' letters in the magazines often show a genuinely critical attitude, however crude its bases and arguments, and acquaintance with the whole body of a given author's work is commonly appealed to, implying some sort of power to make distinctions. Science-fiction readers are addicts, but they are active addicts, positive enthusiasts who are conscious, often all too conscious, of being a specialised minority, highly vocal, and given to banding together in fan clubs.

These clubs are a fascinating feature of American—and British—society, and a full account of them would demand an article to itself. A compressed account would have to start with the foundation of the first clubs in the early '30's and go straight on to the situation today, with groups in a score of major cities and dozens of others: the regional breakdown seems to show that interest is strong in the Midwest and on the West Coast, not so strong in New England and Texas. Many clubs will meet weekly, have a hierarchy of officials, hold organized discussions, and mimeograph or even print a magazine. These fan magazines, or fanzines, appear and disappear at a great rate, but there are pretty sure to be forty or fifty different titles in the current year, with critical, fictional, and gossippy contents. The nomenclature of the field is not reassuring—one fan club is called "The Elves', Gnomes' and Little Men's Science Fiction, Chowder and Marching Society," one of the national federations is "The Little Monsters of America"— but the evidence of energy and serious interest is overwhelming. Every year there are regional conferences and a three-day world convention. There are perhaps twenty fan clubs in Great Britain; I don't know about the Continent. Politically, the clubs are inclined to be progressive, especially on racial questions, and thus reflect a feature of the medium itself: many stories allegorise the theme of discrimination, some treat it directly. At one stage, an immoderate degree of radicalism was attained when a Communist group from Brooklyn, baulked in their attempt to win over the national convention, formed an association for the Political Advancement of Science Fiction—a short-lived organisation, I imagine. I will add as a footnote that apparently fantasy fans are content to march under the banner of their science-fiction friends, who far exceed them in number. However, there must be many who make no distinction between the two forms, and there is evidence that the name "fantasy" carries some kind of unwelcome connotation. Anthony Boucher, when acting as co-editor of *The Magazine of Fantasy and Science Fiction*, reported that "our readers do not prefer science fiction to fantasy, but they think they do," adding that the magazine sold more copies when it carried a science-fiction cover (men in space suits) than when it had a fantasy cover (leprechauns). These facts would strengthen the hand of those who claim that, without being essentially escapist itself, science fiction is often used as a means of escape by its addicts.

Apart from being likely to belong to a fan club, what sort of person reads science fiction? Information about this is profuse, both in bulk and in self-contradiction. A gingerly attempt to reconcile a number of sources gives something like this. Males greatly predominate over females—the proportions given vary between fifteen to one and five to one. The disparity is probably on the decrease. As regards age, the average would come somewhere in the later twenties, with a sprinkling of schoolchildren and a number of veteran fans like the present writer. As for occupation, not unnaturally there is a pronounced technological or scientific bias, with engineers, chemists, research workers, and so on accounting for perhaps forty per cent of readers, though the editor of *Astounding* says that "nearly all" of his readers are "technically trained and employed." Other groups mentioned as numerically important are the non-scientific professions, college students, and the armed forces. As a counter-illustration of occupational diversity, I will just mention an anecdote of de Camp's which tells how a science-fiction writer, happening to visit a New Orleans bordello, found his works so popular with the staff that he was asked to consider himself their guest for the evening. To speculate about the motives and attitudes of readers is precarious, but for what it may be worth I will quote what a number of leading writers have to say about this. Science-fiction readers are "the curious who are looking for stimulation or sensation"; "people with technical training who want fictionalised shop-talk and teen-agers who find glamour and excitement in science"; "ten percent mental juveniles who still like fairy stories, ninety percent chronic nosey-parkers who like having their imaginations stimulated"; "misfits in society, often subversive misfits"; "idealistic, forward-looking, well-read, interested in the arts." Except for the last of these, I detect a welcome lack of reverence here, but on the whole the writers and editors would, I think, echo the boast of the editor of *Astounding* that the medium reaches a large minority of a highly creative and influential section of the nation—the younger technologists. However one regards technologists, there is no doubt that they are important, and since I regard science fiction as a humanising rather than a brutalising force, its circulation among these people strikes me as a hopeful sign.

What sort of person writes science fiction? He—it is "she" once in about fifty times—very seldom depends wholly on the writing of science fiction for his living. The financial rewards are such as to demand either a fantastic output or resignation to modest living standards. Secondary occupations adopted are often concerned with science— teaching and research—or with fiction—sometimes detective stories and/or Westerns, sometimes "general," as they say. A scrutiny of their work and of their own utterances suggests that most of the writers and editors treat their calling with great, sometimes excessive, seriousness. Their claims for the medium often strike a missionary note: science fiction is "the last refuge of iconoclasm in American literature"; it exists "to afford objectivity to the reader, for better consideration of himself and his species"; its function is "to modify the natural conservatism of the creature"; "it helps mankind to be humble." Occasionally, a legitimate pride in a specialised calling unites with an equally understandable desire to see science fiction treated respectfully and produces wild hyperbole. Thus, Reginald Bretnor, an established author and critic, seems to think that science fiction is a much broader field than the whole of the rest of literature; Robert A. Heinlein, an excellent writer, says the stuff "is much more realistic than is most historical and contemporary-scene fiction and is superior to them both," it is "the most difficult of all prose forms," it is "the only form of fiction which stands even a chance of interpreting the spirit of our times." Here one is reminded of the modernist jazz musician claiming that what he plays is superior in subtlety to serious music as well as being more difficult to perform. But to feel that what one is doing is the most important thing in the world is not necessarily undignified, and indeed is perhaps more rather than less likely to lead to good work being done. I have no objection if the science-fiction writer is sometimes a serious and dedicated kind of person.

He would certainly unloose a disapproving frown at my next topic, science fiction on film, television, and radio. The obstacles to successful translation are formidable enough, perhaps resembling, as one commentator sees it, those of converting into the terms of *Life* the values and interests of a class periodical like *The Saturday Review*. In the visual media the effects have got to be lavish: it is no use trying to produce a convincing BEM by fiddling around with slow-motion process shots of newts, and I remember a fearful effort called *The Man from Planet X* in which they made do with just one alien, whose frequent reminders that a lot of his friends from Planet X should be turning up any moment produced only very moderate consternation. Lavishness is costly, and cost must be certain of being recovered; with few exceptions only the most blatant menaces have got on to the screen. With a sad lack of inventiveness, most of the animal kingdom has been successively blown up to giantism and launched against the world: we have had king-sized wasps, ants, spiders, squids, sea-snails, lizards, beetles, birds, and pterodactyls, all doing their best to bring mankind to its knees. *The War of the Worlds*, with excellent Martians and some attempt to set up a logical alien technology, was probably the best of the menace series, if only because it provided a really formidable menace, one that couldn't be polished off with a few rounds of rifle fire. Nowadays, it appears that the boom in science-fiction films has passed—I couldn't find a single one to go to in New York the other day—and without having explored more than a fraction of the possibilities.* The same applies to television: my own survey, which took a long time and was very horrible to do, shows that of five hundred programme-hours studied, only six and one-half, or one and three-tenths per cent, could possibly be classed as science fiction, compared with four and three-tenths per cent of mystery and detective and nearly six per cent of Westerns. Radio is often spoken of as the most promising of the three media for science fiction, but, for my own part, that promise has yet to be honoured: I was spoilt, perhaps, by sitting through *Journey into Space*, an interminable saga on the

---

* The reported sale to the movies of Christopher's *No Blade of Grass* and Arthur C. Clarke's *Childhood's End*, both of them serious and non-sensationalist efforts, perhaps portends a return to the charge in a less frivolous frame of mind.

B.B.C., and by having made rather a mess of a play of my own which was done on the Third Programme, the first science fiction they ever attempted and doubtless the last as well. Noises are good fun all right, but I do not much care for having things "left to my imagination," and the most blood-curdling roars will curdle a good deal less blood, I take it, than the jerkiest king-sized spider on the screen.

From the foregoing hasty and subjective sketch one could at any rate deduce, I think, that on the whole, attempts to present science fiction through mass outlets have failed, though not irretrievably so. It remains only to sum up by considering what use the written medium serves or might serve. I cannot see much justice in the commentators' repeated claim that it sugars the pill of a scientific education: most of the science is wrong anyway, and its amount is such that one might as well be reading Westerns in the hope of finding out about ranching methods. Nor is the medium valuable simply as prophecy: science fiction must in its very profusion seem occasionally to have guessed right, and to have guessed wrong invalidates nothing. Its most important use, I submit, is a means of dramatising social inquiry, as providing a fictional mode in which cultural tendencies can be isolated and judged. To be sure, it does this only at its most ambitious, and then it is often vulgarly presumptuous; but many a trend-hound would be surprised and perhaps mortified to discover how many of his cherished insights are common ground in science fiction. Any Martian survey team would be well advised to read a sample of the stuff before reporting on Terran civilisation.

We today can, in reading the science fiction [stories] of the past, get often a far clearer view of the societies they were written in than from their contemporary "contemporary" fiction and often the non-fictional examinations. Few things reveal so sharply as science fiction the wishes, hopes, fears, inner stresses and tensions of an era, or define its limitations with such exactness.

So says H. L. Gold, editor of *Galaxy Science Fiction* since its foundation in 1950, and so probably able to draw on a larger base for generalisation than most of us. My concern in this section is going to be with those wishes, hopes, and fears as they reveal themselves in contemporary science fiction, rather than with attitudes consciously held and set forth, with emotions rather than with ideas. The line between these two departments is notoriously difficult to draw, and I do not mean to insist too rigorously on a criterion of illogic or unawareness as a justification for mentioning certain factors here instead of later. For the purposes of the present discussion, I shall draw impartially upon science fiction and fantasy, in the belief that the latter sometimes offers material which no wielder of the probe can afford to miss.

This is abundantly true of the group of feelings to which I shall give pride of place: sex. Here indeed the two modes

divide with some sharpness, science fiction evidently re-
strained by its comparatively realistic bias, fantasy sometimes offering sexual fantasy on an uninhibited scale. Space-
opera, to get that out of the way at once, is in its earlier,
Edgar Rice Burroughs form as cool-blooded as a fairy
story: a George Eliot love scene suddenly interpolated
would seem dangerously modern and in questionable taste.
Later space-opera of the galactic-hoodlum sort does, on
occasion, borrow a bit of sadism from its private-eye ana-
logue, but for the most part it remains hardly less decorous
than Superman. Science fiction similarly unshackles the
libido but seldom, often appearing to go out of its way to
be chaste. *Amazing Stories*, the outlet as you may recall
for Holly Kendall's admittedly odd dealings with her trans-
migrated father, recently published a story called "The
Blonde from Space," with a cover-picture showing two
space-suited heroes in a state of emotional collapse and
an open-mouthed siren billowing up in the background. The
circulation of *Amazing Stories* may have gone up a little
that month, but the story itself is Sunday-school reading,
even though the blonde turns out to be a very malignant
alien in disguise. If one's probe might be inclined to linger
interestedly at this point, it would I think have to pass by
in view of the non-physical nature of the malignity and the
resolute way it is kept off-stage. We should almost be justified in demanding that at least the lovely violet eyes should
fill with a strange non-human gleam, as any writer in *Amazing* would surely put it if so minded, but not even that much
is given us. In general, the nature and direction of sexual
interest in science fiction is almost oppressively normal,
more so than in any comparable mode except the Western.
Its amount, however, is small, a fact bemoaned by many a
commentator, and the tone in which it does get mentioned
is often self-righteous. There is usually some kind of bor-

dello attached to Marsport, and a hint of something more elaborate and fanciful in the vacation resort on Procyon IX, but the hero will go there simply for a drink, or to observe superciliously, or in pursuit of some unamiable character who really likes it there, and while I agree that a lofty attitude is a favourite self-excuse for salacity and so on, effects of that kind need elbow-room: our hero will normally have passed out or started shooting before the Procyonian lovelies have had time to turn around. When, again, a science-fiction writer is portraying a decadent society, as he so frequently does, we are lucky if we miss some generalised account, or at least a mention, of reprehensible sexual exuberance. No wife who finds her husband addicting himself to science fiction need fear that he is in search of an erotic outlet, anyway not an overt one. We know, or at least are constantly being told, that people are given to betraying sexual attitudes when they are apparently talking about something else, and the role of a spaceship as a male symbol, though not, or not so much, the role of its inside as a female one, has before now been the subject of supposedly rational discourse. I should not like to discourage the use of these methods, and I am only being autobiographical if I say that what a man thought he was saying is often more interesting than what he might have really been saying: let complication thrive. Acknowledged discussions of sexual questions, offered as subject matter by science-fiction writers, I reserve for a later section.

Sexual fantasy in fantasy, as I put it, presents a totally different picture, one which might well blanch the cheek of our hypothetical wife. I select for investigation a novella called "The Circus of Dr. Lao," first published in 1935, but reprinted as the title story in a collection of 1956 edited by Ray Bradbury, himself a celebrated writer of both fantasy and science fiction. The narrative first gives an account, thin in verisimilitude, of how the people of a small town in Arizona reacted to the arrival from nowhere in particular of a circus advertising among its attractions a unicorn, a satyr, a sphinx, a chimera, a werewolf, a mermaid, and other familiar novelties. The rest of the story treats in great detail of the remarkably orgiastic show put on by these creatures, with assistance from one or two members of the audience. We are offered flagellation and rape in chief, with bestiality, pederasty, and voyeurism thrown in, plus a good deal of sweat and musk and that kind of thing. An intellectual top-dressing is provided by Dr. Lao's erudite lectures on the histories of the various participants, and we find at the end of the story a fifteen-page appendix, consisting of sardonic quasi-epigrams about all the entities mentioned, the whole rounded off with a list of thirteen internal inconsistencies or unsolved questions: "What did Mumbo Jumbo do with the fair-haired Nordic girl?" and so on. What is actually being propounded in this work is apparently that people are often attracted by shocking and nasty things, and inevitably it is the local school-mistress who responds to the satyr's lack of ceremony. I must admit I find it all unedifying, or even what I might roughly describe as unpleasant. I have nothing against pornography, perhaps I should explain, but in my old-fashioned way I like it straight, uncontaminated with cruelty and disgust. These two qualities appear and even run riot in a good deal of modern fantasy, more often in what is not overtly a sexual form, though I am quite willing to entertain the idea that they will always have sexual undertones.

Immediately following the Dr. Lao story comes "The Pond," by Nigel Kneale, a British writer who has since scripted two rather, but not excessively, horrific science-fiction films. In "The Pond," a nasty old man who spends

most of his time stuffing frogs is got hold of by the sur-
viving frogs and stuffed by them. A single guffaw will ex-
orcise most of the spell of that one, but one pauses to note
that, apart from reeds and such, the main form of stuffing
used on the old man is slime, a substance admittedly
likely to be plentiful in any place where frogs live, but
also significantly common in works of this nature. Stories
about evisceration, or mutilation in general, once fairly
common in science fiction of the mad-scientist school, are
now a settled ingredient of fantasy. Ray Bradbury has a
couple of this kind. In "The Man Upstairs," a nasty man-like
creature, probably, but not certainly, an alien, is deprived
of his internal organs, which turn out to be geometrical
gelatinous hunks, and then sewn up again like the frog
expert. The performer in this case, typically for Bradbury,
and not untypically for all such tales, is an eleven-year-old
boy, who again typically says, on being promised a vacation to forget it all, "Why should it be bad? I don't see
anything bad. I don't feel bad." The other story, "Skeleton,"
introduces a man who suffers from aching bones and at the
end is entirely deprived of them by some sort of creature
of man-like appearance but apparently capable at need of
climbing down through people's mouths and eating their
skeletons from within. The story closes with the victim's
wife arriving home:

Many times as a little girl Clarisse had run on the beach sands,
stepped on a jellyfish and screamed. It was not so bad, finding an intact, gelatin-skinned jellyfish in one's living room.
One could step back from it.

It was when the jellyfish *called you by name* . . .

Quite jolly, really, though again perhaps lacking in uplift.
I confess I don't quite know the received interpretation of
such matters, but I feel there must be one. I should not

like to give the impression, finally, that the field of fantasy consists entirely of impracticable horrors. There are plenty of perfectly sedate accounts of pacts with demons and so on, witches of routine malignity, and cordially disposed pixies treated of with nothing worse than appalling whimsicality. And I do not want to suggest that it is somehow undesirable to read or write stories about frogs stuffing old men or people being turned into jellyfishes. But the impression lingers that a good look through the mailing lists of the fantasy magazines would amply repay anybody setting up in business as an analyst.

I turn now to a far less tangible group of feelings, those associated with insecurity or the desire for security; I exclude from consideration rational fears or warnings about immediate practical possibilities like an all-out nuclear war, merely observing in passing that if a great deal of science fiction is concerned with the aftermath of such a war, this need not be explained as pessimism or fatalism, rather as a plot-manoeuvre for setting up a story about mutations or tribal society. A non-rational sense of insecurity can be disentangled from several favourite myths or recurring situations in science fiction. One of these is obviously that of the eventual extinction of the human race. The agencies involved are variously imagined. Man will be destroyed by an alien invasion, but the malignant alien is passing out of fashion, and any unexpected visitors are more likely to have missionary motives. If they arrive too late to find mankind still a going concern, there will be awed speculation about the departed great ones. Man will perish in the course of some natural disaster: a new and more severe Ice Age, a plague that attacks directly or via the destruction of plant life, a comet invading the solar system, though all these, in their different ways, are likely to be averted by science or luck. More interestingly, the human race will be ousted by another form of terrestrial life, an enlightened kind of rat in one case, more often an unenlightened and formidable strain of ants, an obvious symbol, I suppose, for the society that may in fact compete successfully with our own, being highly organised, unindividualistic, ruthless, unemotional, inexhaustible in numbers, incomprehensible, and whatever else it may be or seem to be. There is also a group of stories about the doom of man that deliberately attribute no rational cause and foresee no kind of future. One of the best of these is Arthur C. Clarke's "The Nine Billion Names of God." Here, a Tibetan lamasery buys from the Americans a giant computer to compile a list that shall include all the nine billion names referred to. When this has been done, the lama explains, the human race will have completed the purpose for which it was created. The two technicians on loan, their mission virtually over, are riding down to catch the plane home when they notice that the stars are beginning to go out. Similarly, Robert Sheckley's "The Mountain Without a Name" is about a planetary expedition that suffers a series of disasters, each in itself explicable, but together utterly defeating the law of averages. A speech near the end, regrettably rhetorical in style, explains that man is a presumptuous jellyfish that the cosmos has got tired of. A radio conversation with Earth establishes that natural causes have brought about a good deal all over the place, including the sinking of Australia.

These two stories, as well as being pretty doom-laden, presumably also allegorise certain irrational feelings about where knowledge may land you if you aren't careful, a theme I shall take up again in a moment. First, however, I want to look at a specialised group of stories involving the notion that human existence might, through a minor flaw in the system, suddenly be revealed as some kind of puppet-show. This is sometimes handled lightly enough, as in another piece by Robert Sheckley, "The Impacted Man," in which the hero finds himself back in the Stone Age whenever he tries to leave his apartment. It transpires that this "time flaw" has been caused by the use of shoddy atoms on the part of the universe-constructor, who is evidently some kind of cosmic landscape-gardener. The flaw is repaired without the entire galaxy having to be rebuilt. This is a joke to Sheckley, but other treatments of the idea are more sombre. In Fredric Brown's "Come and Go Mad," for instance, human life and especially warfare are conceived of as a game played by parts of an organism against other parts of itself. On being shown a single cell of this organism, an ant crawling over the woodwork, the hero goes mad, as well he might. Another story, "Compounded Interest," treats human history as the by-product of the attempts of a time-traveller to raise the money to build a time-machine to go back in time to start raising the money again. Variations on this theme include a story by Frederik Pohl, in which a man finds out that he and all his fellow-townspeople are minute androids being used in an advertising experiment, and there is a fantasy piece by Ray Bradbury where human fates are determined by a real man with a scythe cutting down real wheat somewhere in the Middle West. The dread of finding that one is being used, as in the Pohl story, reappears in many places where only specific characters, not human beings at large, are thus exploited, and certainly such alien malignity as is still manifested nearly always foregoes physical attack and concentrates on domination of the mind: see Robert A. Heinlein's novel *The Puppet Masters*. Some of these treatments, then, seem to be allegorising a fear of the loss of individuality and free will; others are perhaps better summed up by the remark of a character in Alfred Bester's *Demolished Man*:

"When life gets tough, you tend to take refuge in the idea that it's all make-believe, a giant hoax." Possibly I should say here that I claim no novelty for the themes of these stories, nor any particular literary merit in their treatment; but to have to ignore such considerations is a price one pays for deciding to wield the analyst's probe.

Going back now to feelings about the possible dangers of science and technology, I alluded in a previous section to the Frankenstein myth and to one or two of its descendants in contemporary science fiction. There are, of course, innumerable stories about robots getting out of control, but their behaviour is more often merely eccentric, posing a problem of diagnosis, than effectively hostile. There is here and there even a complacency about man's ability to keep his creations under physical control, and in some places I detect a tendency to regard electronic behaviour as "better," because more rational and predictable, than human. This idea is delightfully burlesqued in a story by Philip K. Dick, "The Defenders," in which the human race is living underground while the robots fight the war on the surface. Although the latter keep sending down film reports of tremendous battles and huge destruction wrought upon the enemy by the new weapons the men spend all their time inventing, nothing decisive seems to happen. No human being has been allowed up top for decades: too dangerous, say the robots. When a party of men does get to ground level, they find that the robots, having called off hostilities the moment the last hatch was sealed, and agreeing that mankind could never be trusted not to start things again, have been spending their time faking their reports as interestingly as possible. On the whole, machinery as such does not seem to terrify science-fiction writers: there is just one exceptional story, Theodore Sturgeon's *Killdozer*, about a malignant alien intelligence taking over, oddly enough, a bulldozer during airfield-construction operations, but this recalls less the nightmare of a protoplasmic creature in a world of metal than the feelings of a man trying to start his car on a cold morning. It is the moral and spiritual dangers of a technological civilisation that exercise these writers, and whereas their statement of these must wait until a later section, their modes of escape from such a civilisation, turning up significantly often in stories otherwise quite unconcerned with the problem, can appropriately be considered now.

I am aware that nostalgia for a rural way of life is not confined to writers of science fiction, but its volume and intensity in that mode are tremendous. It goes right back, clearly, to the primitive days, to William Morris, to Richard Jefferies's modern-sounding romance, *After London*, to Wells's "Story of the Days to Come," which shows, in a different contemporary style, the well-intentioned city dwellers unable to cope with the rigours of the countryside. Since Jefferies, it may be remarked, few such writers have shown much grasp of what rural life actually entails: these are the velleities of those long in populous city pent, as so much feeling about the country notoriously is. But the desire to get out in those woods and hear those birds singing, however notional, is clearly there. If we had enough sense, we'd be doing it now: this is an almost explicit minor theme of Poul Anderson's *Brain Wave*—the Earth comes out of an electronic field that inhibits intelligence, and the IQs have hardly finished rising before urban civilisation is quietly being superseded. Clifford D. Simak's novel *Ring Around the Sun*, after a brisk run-through of citified evils, takes its hero off to a potential paradise of greenery, not on a distant Earth-type planet but, obviously of set purpose, on an unspoiled replica of Earth in some extra dimension immediately adjacent to our own, and the journey is made not by any technological wizardry but by a semi-mystical ritual involving the hero's memories of his rural childhood. The anti-urban theme is common in Simak, a prolific and markedly emotional writer who has become a kind of science-fiction poet laureate of the countryside, plus what I should guess to be characteristically American notions about the practical virtues of the folks who live there. Examples of Simak's syndrome could be multiplied: I will just note that they are very rare in British writing in this field. The only instance I have encountered, John Wyndham's "Time to Rest," shows us an aged Earthman, perhaps on the point of throwing in his lot with a family of rustic Martians, but feeling that there was a good deal more to life on Earth, now unfortunately an exploded planet. A story by Fredric Brown, "The Waveries," idealises small-town American life of the horse-and-buggy days; the waveries are a type of inconvenient but non-malevolent alien life who feed on electricity and so bring all mechanised amenities to a standstill. The hard-drinking hero switches to beer and takes up playing cornet in the town band. The last story I need quote here, "Of Missing Persons," first appeared in *Good Housekeeping* in 1955 and is by an author who has yet to make his name. Like "Legacy of Terror," the entymology piece, this is one of those things that offer themselves for analysis with an almost suspicious readiness.

The first-person hero, Charlie Ewell, on recommendation from a stranger met in a bar, goes to a travel bureau and asks the man to help him to escape. "From what?" the man asks. Charlie hesitates; he's "never put it into words before." Then:

"From New York, I'd say. And cities in general. From worry. And fear. And the things I read in my newspapers. From lone-

liness . . . From never doing what I really want to do or having much fun. From selling my days just to stay alive. From
life itself—the way it is today, at least." I looked straight at
him and said softly, "From the world."

With this established, the agency man, who looks "the way
ministers should look . . . the way all fathers should look,"
shows Charlie a brochure about Verna, evidently a planet
of some sort. The name is a back-formation from "vernal,"
presumably, rather than a tribute to old Jules. Charlie gazes
dumbly at photographs of almost virgin forest dotted with
log cabins.

I don't know how you knew this, but you realised, staring at
that forest-covered valley, that this was very much the way
America once looked when it was new . . . you were seeing
what people, the last of them dead over a century ago, had once
looked at in Kentucky and Wisconsin and the old Northwest. . . .
Under that picture was another, of six or eight people on a
beach. . . . You knew—I tell you, you *knew*—that they liked
their work, all of them, whatever it was . . . it was a place
where no one worried or was ever afraid . . . these people were
happy . . . they always would be, and they knew it.

Charlie asks the agency man what the people do.

"They work; everyone does. . . . They simply live their lives
doing what they like . . . they work at whatever it is they really
want to do."

"And if there isn't anything they really want to do?"

. . . "There is always something, for everyone, that he really
wants to do. It's just that here there is so rarely time to find
out what it is."

He adds reassuringly that although life is simple it isn't
rough: no cars or television, but washing machines and
modern bathrooms—a very common reservation, this, on
the part of the simple-life champions, for after all any fool

can be uncomfortable. With a side-glance at the pictures of
the inside of the cabins—"furnished in a kind of Early
American style, except that it looked—authentic"—Charlie
applies for a ticket to Verna, but never gets there; he loses
his faith just at the wrong moment and then it's too late;
you don't get a second chance.

This is clearly fantasy, even in the technical sense: you
don't travel to Verna, you just sort of find yourself there.
I have quoted freely from "Of Missing Persons" because
it is one of those stories that seem to anthologise within
themselves dozens of other stories and pieces of stories from
all over, not only inside fantasy or science fiction. This
trend-hound's Christmas dinner shows the longing for escape
in as raw a form as I have seen anywhere. The particular
kind of escape looked for is—I need not recapitulate—rural
in setting, even if summer-visitor rural; it involves some
dimly visualised social group in which everybody likes
everybody else; and there is this point about doing the kind
of job you enjoy—a sole criterion, since the worthiness of
the job, equally with financial reward for it, never reaches
discussion. One remarks the omission, from the earlier parts
of the story, of even a perfunctory attempt to show Charlie
actually in his job at the bank and hating the manager or
the customers, in the same way that another type of story
doesn't bother to explain why the space-ship is going into
space: such things are given. Omissions from the later stages
are more striking. No kind of sexuality seems to be expected
in this kind of Arcady: earlier versions may have been
pretty replete with pipes and timbrels and wild ecstasy, but
there are none here. As I read, I was expecting any moment
a reference to some young lady with at least a breath of
springtime in her hair and a hint of laughter in her steady
grey eyes, imagined as sitting in at one of the barbecues,
but even she failed to materialise. Although Charlie Ewell

will never rank as one of my favourite characters in fiction, and although I should probably agree with most of what that bank manager would have said about him, it has to be admitted that his desires do not include any kind of self-aggrandisement. He may be enervated and self-indulgent, but he is neither lazy nor irresponsible. The worst that could be said of him is that he takes happiness too seriously.

Without bringing up—for the moment—the question whether science fiction is an escapist medium, I might offer a word about one other apparent form of escape within it. It needs to be made clear that, whereas it might appear to an inquirer that to get into a space-ship and travel to the rim of the galaxy is a fairly efficient method of escaping from problems at home, yet it is not so viewed inside the field. If anybody does sign on because of a quarrel or a broken home, the crew will regard him with a professional resentment, much as a sergeant of machine-guns in the Foreign Legion might react to the presence of an English aristocrat in the latest intake. Whatever we may think it really is or would be, space is viewed as the forefront of active life, the region where the future is made rather than talked about or run away from. This is not to say that such a prospect, much less that of continuing technological innovation in general, is made the occasion for unconditional optimism, rather the contrary, for as we shall see, science fiction is becoming in part a literature of scepticism and deflation. But it remains true that the medium is, if not optimistic, at any rate strongly activist in its attitudes. It may show, and often does show, human kind groaning in chains of its own construction, but nearly always with the qualification that those chains can be broken if people try hard enough. Any purely personal solution, any withdrawal to the cultivation of one's hydroponic garden, is likely to prove unpopular, and should a rural paradise become available, no science-fiction hero worth his salt will rest until he has got most of his friends admitted as well. What I mean by an activist temper will perhaps emerge from a consideration of two important science-fiction novels not generally read as such. Orwell's *Nineteen Eighty-Four*, you will be glad to hear, went down very well in science-fiction circles, and has been assimilated into the medium, as it were, being offered for paper-back sale in a series that includes *The Demolished Man* and Heinlein's *Puppet Masters*: "The tyrannical, terrifying world of 1984," the blurb says, "—the end-product of forces already at work today"; an interesting sidelight on how publishers feel science fiction is read. Some of Orwell's ideas and even nomenclature—"Big Brother" and "Thought Police," for instance—seem on the verge of passing into the general furniture of the nasty utopia. But when O'Brien says to Winston: "If you want a picture of the future, imagine a boot stamping on a human face—forever," thus summing up the book, a conclusion is being reached which, whether plausible or not, or hysterical or not, almost no orthodox science-fiction writer would admit. Similarly, if we can imagine *Brave New World* rewritten by Anthony Boucher or Frederik Pohl, we could expect (as well as a little more narrative from time to time) an early scene showing a group of technicians working out a scheme for secretly subjecting all the Beta, Gamma, Delta, and Epsilon embryos to Alpha conditioning, just as a start. And the Savage might die at the hands of Mustapha Mond's police force, but he would never commit suicide.

This confidence in human character and abilities, though often of the kind a headmaster says he has in you in the course of a denunciation and threat-session, can at other times seem almost excessive. I have said that an occasional robot story shows complacency in its assumption that not much can go wrong. A robot piece by Henry Kuttner and

C. L. Moore, "Home There's No Returning," though things
go wrong quite violently, points in something of the same
direction. For the purposes of winning the current war, a
vast peripatetic computer has been constructed, incorporat-
ing the novelty that, unlike ordinary computers but like
men, it will make decisions on insufficient data. Immediately upon being activated it goes psychotic, and most of
the story consists of the various attempts to calm it down.
When it has at last been persuaded to switch itself off, the
general in charge, previously half dead from exhaustion,
bucks up wonderfully. He reflects that the robot

couldn't act on partial knowledge. No machine could. You
couldn't expect machines to face the unknown. Only human
beings can do that. Steel isn't strong enough. Only flesh and
blood can do it, and go on.

"What do I mean, *only* flesh and blood?" he asked.

I should not like to call this complacency, but it does bear
witness in a highly representative fashion to a boundless
self-confidence, a feeling that if humanity to itself do rest
but true, no situation will be too tough and no problem too
difficult. It is almost obligatory that when Galactic Headquarters get the news that space-ships have been detected
leaving Sol III, everybody should hold up his tentacles in
astonishment: "Impossible!" Vora will say; "they've only
had the internal combustion engine for a century or so."
For "human pride" in this context we can often, of course,
read "Western pride" or "American pride," and though the
cause adduced for such pride may be skill or toughness, it
may also be resiliency and humour. In "Late Night Final,"
by Eric Frank Russell, a British writer, an invading force
of absurdly militaristic but not actually malignant aliens is
assimilated by the villagers who live near the landing site.
This may be taken simply as a victory of human over alien,

or rural over urban, but it is clearly also democratic over totalitarian. To revert, however: the outset of the space age and the immense technological effort involved in it are obviously the propelling force of much science fiction to-day, and a main cause or occasion of self-congratulatory feeling. Most, if not all, readers and writers of science fiction would go a good deal of the way with Arthur Clarke's scientist on the moon, to whom the conquest of space repre-sents a new Renaissance. This, for me, is as it should be, though there are a lot of other things that also should be.

Science and scientists, as one might expect, come in for a major share of the plaudits. When anything goes wrong, from the death of an alien diplomat to the Earth being blown into the sun, it is never a scientist's fault. The poli-ticians have refused to allow the taking of some necessary precaution, or the generals have been demanding action before all the tests were complete, or the business tycoons have put the model into production without waiting for the results of the pilot scheme. Again and again the god-dam administrators insist on interfering, instead of leaving things to the men on the job. In *The Black Cloud*, by Fred Hoyle, a British astronomer of, I believe, considerable standing, a first-order catastrophe apparently threatens mankind. The scientists set up a project to deal with it and keep the politicians out, grinning away whenever some Washington or London fool fulminates over the telephone or is ignominiously turned away from the front gate at bayonet-point. In a far less intelligently written story, Max Ehrlich's *The Big Eye*, an American one this time, the good old Earth-destroying comet turns up again, only for once it's just going to miss the Earth. By a piece of blood-curdling arrogance, the scientists of all nations decide to pretend it will just hit, a manoeuvre fully endorsed by the author and aimed at reducing international tension and so forth. Now I don't like goddam administrators, but I like this kind of behaviour even less; a scientist is fine in his place and only there; you know the arguments. Anyway, here is one the trend-hounds ought to get on to, and with despatch. Science fiction is, if you like, a hilariously unreliable preview of science, but is apt to be much nearer the mark about scientists.

A long way down the ladder from science and scientists come art and artists. Throughout science fiction, art is mentioned in tones of tremendous respect and with a frequency not even paralleled in women's-magazine stories. Typically, however, art is a dead-and-gone thing; its relics in an ancient city of the extinct Martian race, a Ray Bradbury instance, form a sufficient reason for not tearing down that city, but it is rare to find living art, contemporaneous with the story, treated as much more than either an excuse for ingenuity in the colour-organ, perfume-ballet vein, or something of the same standing as interior decoration, a background accompaniment to civilised living. It would take a bold man to construct a twenty-third-century poem—even Robert Graves in *Watch the North Wind Rise* (English title: *Seven Days in New Crete*) only gave us the product of a future Metaphysical revival—but I should like to see it attempted more often. It may be significant that the only serious guesses at future art that I have seen make it into something rather horrible. Clifford Simak, in "Shadow Show," invents a kind of puppet-theatre with full audience participation, since they project all the action from their minds; this turns out to be the method of creating life artificially that human beings have long been seeking. This makes the story a quite effective modern variation on an old nightmare about the literary imagination, but it does seem to foresee a certain decadence. Kuttner and Moore's "Vintage Season" hypothesises a synaesthetic art, apparently largely musical, which yet incorporates physical nauseas and televisual views of actual historical scenes—nasty ones. (The artist of the future, incidentally, often comes off better than his works: in the conformist utopia he is a favourite choice for the deviate, the valuable social misfit.)

I want now to take up an earlier point of mine about human self-confidence. The penetration of space, as I said, is seen as a natural and healthy development, but there is a good deal of understandable self-questioning about what may eventually be found there. Although misgivings about the piety of plumbing the universe would be regarded as obscurantist and Victorian, feelings about the littleness of man do find frequent expression, and I do not refer simply to decorative passages in which the young space-cadet gazes with awe upon the stellar immensities: that is the cue for an instability in the atomic pile to become apparent. I also referred earlier to the wise and kind aliens who have taken over so signally from the man-eating, death-ray-dealing aliens of twenty and more years ago. It is in this way that emotions of humility and reverence most commonly make their appearance in science fiction, and I should not fight hard against a diagnosis of these as religious, or at least religiose. Religion in the straightforward sense is treated thematically in the fantasy novels of C. S. Lewis and of Charles Williams, which are exceptions to many rules; the first half and the end of James Blish's *A Case of Conscience* form a lonely science-fiction example. Another is a story by Anthony Boucher, "The Quest for Saint Aquin," in which the saint turns out to be a robot. Since the robot's brain is by definition perfectly logical, its embracing of Roman Catholicism is understood as inaugurating a new ecclesiastical era. On the other side of the question, one of Isaac Asimov's robots becomes a religious maniac, logically deducing its superiority to non-

rational humanity. In "For I Am a Jealous People," by
Lester del Rey, God withdraws his covenant from men and
bestows it on the aliens who are invading Earth, upon
which the hero, a minister, decides that the war must go
on and that this time God has picked an opponent his own
size, a remarkably thorough-going version of the human
pride I was talking about. These uses of religious subject
matter are, as I said, exceptional*; an attitude of casual
disrespect is far more common. It is as if religion were
tacitly agreed to have an earthly, or Terrene, limitation
when the scale of human activity has become galactic. Even
at moments of extreme terror and painful wonder, it is not
the resort of characters for whom our whole-hearted approval is solicited. When the sun seems about to turn into
a nova, when the alien space-fleet closes in, when famine
and pestilence follow in the wake of a nuclear war, prophets
and fanatics impose themselves on the rabble while the
scientists set their jaws and get on with the job. Organised
religion among alien subject-peoples is to be treated, where
possible, with the same sort of respect as their dietary
habits, but will probably come in handy if taken over and
used as a means of manipulating them. To credit a priest-
hood, usually portrayed as enjoying much temporal mag-
nificence, with such a discreditable role is not, I think, to

* They may have started becoming less exceptional. Alongside many
stories embodying a wishy-washy loving-kindness only generically Christian, we find a few that envisage a future ecclesiastical revival in
favourable, or at least non-hostile, terms. The latest of these, Walter
Miller, Jr.'s *Canticle for Leibowitz*, shows us the Church as the guardian
of knowledge in a barbarous atomic aftermath. Although containing
some amusing satire on monastic self-dedication (the copyist section
spends half its time elaborately illuminating copies of twentieth-century
wiring diagrams that nobody understands), this novel has passages of
what seem to me to be genuine religious conviction not devoid of
impressiveness. The kind of religion described—in full and affectionate
detail—is strongly hierarchical Roman Catholicism, as in this kind of
story it invariably is: a rich bone for the trend-hound.

be mistaken for anything so directed as satire on our own religious institutions, but it does indicate that, as one might expect, the Church cannot be said to have captured the higher reaches of the science-fiction imagination.

To revert once more: religious or quasi-religious feelings in the medium attach themselves to the super-intelligent or super-moral alien power. This emerges most strongly in the work of Clifford Simak, who as well as being its nature poet comes nearest, by a familiar linkage, to being science fiction's religious writer. In "Contraption," a small boy with nasty foster-parents encounters a small space-ship with two nice aliens in it. Communication is established:

They reached out to him and seemed to take him in their arms and hold him tight against them and Johnny went down on his knees without knowing it and held out his arms to the things that lay there among the broken bushes and cried out to them, as if there was something there that he might grasp and hold— some comfort that he had always missed and longed for and now finally had found.

Johnny gives them his only possession, a jackknife, and they give him a jewel that turns the nasty foster-parents into nice foster-parents. The pattern reappears in "Kindergarten," in which the aliens set up an immense building for the instruction of representatives of the human race. In the course of these operations they demonstrate a technique for reducing all military weapons to impotence and incidentally, but quite predictably, cure the hero's cancer. We last see him in the classroom on the first morning, holding the heroine's hand and waiting for the arrival of the Teacher. (I might say here that nothing is more typical of science fiction than that it presents what are at any rate interesting ideas, and sometimes even original ones, in terms of electrifying banality.) However, this is Simak's theme, but it is not only his. The alien culture that is wiser, rather than simply more knowledgeable, than man's turns up in innumerable stories; similarly, the universal brotherhood so frequently offered humanity will turn out to have its moral and spiritual, as well as its merely political, implications. I can round off this point by referring to a story by Algis Budrys, "Silent Brother," which inverts a common theme of horrific science fiction. The hero finds an alien intelligence living symbiotically in his own body and mind. The alien benefits by locomotion and the power to manipulate; the human being has his missing teeth grown back for him —the physical aspect is again indispensable—and experiences the sense of a "gentle, intelligent being" within him, giving him "sanity and rest, tranquillity and peace," seeing to it that "age is calm, and death is always a falling asleep." The hero would not be a science-fiction hero if he did not see to it that silent brothers were made available to anybody who felt the need of one. This is perhaps no more than hankering after a kind of super-confidence pill, but I am not one who can allot priorities among rods and staffs and comforters.

It will be seen that, in general, no clear-cut, unified picture emerges. In particular, there is an apparent conflict between notions of self-confidence and self-questioning, but these are notions that have always been able to co-exist merrily in different areas of interest within the human skull, or even in the same areas. It is a poor mind that is never in conflict. Let me sum up by saying that, if any sort of moral or social preview can be extricated from the less fully argued attitudes of science fiction, that preview strikes me as largely a reassuring one.* That insensate denial of

---

* Its least reassuring feature is an excessive reverence for science. No matter how often we are shown or told that disaster may result from unchecked scientific discovery, the general feeling seems to be that the

rationality which is notoriously to be found in much 'tec and thriller writing, and even in some contemporary literature of the main stream, is rare in this field. Perhaps there is actually an excessive respect for reason here, but whatever may be said in favour of too little reason as a choice of evils in our private life, in the public domain we ought always to choose too much.

scientific attitude will and should take precedence over any other kind. Non-fictional treatment of the topic in the magazines is likely to press for more scientific education and relegate the humanities to the status of a low-priority appendage. There is, however, remarkably little clear thinking on this subject at any level.

On the other side of the picture, it is worth noting that "reassuringness" of the kind I mean can be found even in the worst magazines. That fearful Third Monster Issue of *Super-Science Fiction* contains one ill-written tale in which a commander sacrifices his life in the course of protecting an alien race from commercial exploitation, and another of similar merit that castigates an interstellar spy for murdering, in the line of duty, a number of repulsive, but gentle and honourable, alien officials. It would take a very odd kind of person to be much uplifted by these pieties, but pieties they remain.

Having given some account of the less fully argued attitudes to be found in science fiction, I intend now to examine the role of the medium as an instrument of social
diagnosis and warning. In doing so I shall select certain
works for more detailed discussion than hitherto, even to
the point where some appraisal of their literary qualities
becomes possible. This may seem a dangerous undertaking
for one who evidently believes that science fiction is suit-
able reading matter for adults, but it is a necessary task.
Division of the material into categories of subject matter
is not easy, for a writer who sets up a satirical utopia in
the hope of isolating certain tendencies in technology, say,
will not and should not overlook the economic and political
and ethical tendencies that would accompany the technological. I shall consider myself justified, then, in wander-
ing now and then from the subject-category under discussion, in the belief that this is a fairer procedure than chop-
ping a book up into arbitrary sections.

The first category, offered first because it separates itself
at a glance from what will follow, is sex. As I remarked
before, science fiction is a literature in which specific sexual
interest of the kind familiar to us from other literatures,
manifested in terms of interplay between individual characters, is rare, conventional, and thin. Nothing better typifies

87

the medium, however, than that this material poverty should co-exist with a readiness to theorise and debate. Science fiction—and this is one of the better arguments advanced by its detractors—is always more at home with generalisations than with particularities. It naturally accommodates, therefore, a novel of a forensic disposition like Philip Wylie's *The Disappearance*. The datum here is that at the same instant of time all the men in the world disappear from the point of view of the women, and all the women from the point of view of the men. The author very sensibly offers no rationalistic explanation for this untoward novelty, nor for its eventual cessation, a factor which would induce us to label the book as fantasy rather than science fiction were it not for the severely reasonable and sober tone in which everything is transacted. The major defect of the performance, apart from a strategical error whereby much of the material is presented as author-comment rather than being dramatised, lies in the fact that the sensibility exhibited is not really adequate to the complexity of the sexual and philosophical issues raised. But there are comparatively few of us whose sensibility would be adequate to an examination not only of the part played by sex in contemporary society, but of the whole inner nature of sexual difference, such as we find here, and I find it hard to blame Wylie for being ambitious at a time when so many novelists of the main stream, out of a proper and yet misplaced sense of their inadequacy, are biting off less than they can chew. Furthermore, even at his most essayistic, Wylie shows none of that complacent indifference to his reader, that unquenchable enjoyment of the sound of his own voice, which characterises the "great" novelist. He diversifies his theme with a number of routine attacks on the American social scene, routine not in that they are perfunctory or unimaginative but in that a writer in the field who foregoes this kind of opportunity is putting himself in the same laughable category as a novelist of Army life who neglects to include a beating-up by the military police. However: the most interesting parts of *The Disappearance* are not the theorisings on American materialism, nor even the amiable satire on women, who naturally go on dressing up to compete with one another just as they did when there were men about, but the conclusions eventually reached about the imperfection with which our society embodies the psychological differences between men and women. Wylie thinks that the sexes are far less divided in this way than we all make them out to be, that an ideology which turns one sex into a norm of humanity, and the other into a divergence from that norm, has got a lot to be said against it. I myself feel inclined to applaud this conclusion, since female emancipation, like education, socialism, and Christianity, strikes me as one of those interesting ideas that have never actually been tried out. But my point here is not to debate the merits of Wylie's thesis, nor even of his arguments, but simply to suggest that, as things are, the only kind of fiction in which they could be deployed is science fiction. However dull a dramatised essay may be, it is unlikely to be as dull as an undramatised one. *The Disappearance* is four hundred pages long.

I pass over a handful of wistful and momentary pieties about anti-feminist prejudice on the part of selection boards for planetary survey teams—pieties contradicted by the enthusiasm with which the authors get down to describing an exclusively male society—and come to a pair of works that by a curious chance envisage the same unlikely situation, an entirely female world reproducing itself by parthenogenesis. As far as I can determine, the two were written simultaneously somewhere about three years ago; in any event, only the starting point is the same. Both

authors are British, a further coincidence with the merit of
ruling out any talk about the death-wish of the American
male. The longer piece, a novel by Charles Eric Maine
called *World Without Men*, is concerned with two points,
of which the minor, but far more interesting, unfortunately
handled as an antecedent to the main story, is that a completely certain and pleasant method of contraception would
lead to the abandonment of marriage and beyond that to
the breakup of the social pattern as we know it. This in
itself would be the subject for a novel, but Maine evades
it, substituting some run-of-the-mill cloak-and-daggery,
some satire on commercial research and promotion which
is too amusing to be run-of-the-mill but is parenthetical, and
some sadly unscientific explanatory talk about Nature com-
pensating for induced female sterility by arranging for more
and more girl babies to be born, just as she arranges for
more boy babies during wartime: as far as I know, which
means that Maine ought to know it too, what is at work in
the latter case is not "Nature," but the tendency of young
parents to produce male offspring. The other theme of
World Without Men is that a perfectly stable but unnatural
society, such as the unisexual one here portrayed, ought to
be turned towards the natural, even at the price of disorder
and great personal unhappiness. Thus we find one of the
girl scientists facing the life of a fugitive in order to protect
the experimentally produced male baby which the security
council wants destroyed. This active dislike of any polity
which prohibits change is widespread to the point of being
almost axiomatic in contemporary science fiction, and I
regard this as a hopeful sign, more hopeful certainly than
the example of Huxley's Savage, who, as I noted earlier,
merely sits about thinking how nice freedom would be. I
would not, of course, dispute the fact that Maine, like his
colleagues, is apt to err by oversimplification.

The other unisexual piece, John Wyndham's novella "Consider Her Ways," is less activist, less rambling, and far more plausible. What set things on foot here was not Nature, but a mutated virus originally developed to kill off the brown rat that turned out to kill off men as well, leaving women almost unaffected. As the title indicates, what develops is a rigidly stratified society recalling the ant-hill, and into this, as a result of some experiments with hallucinogenic drugs, there strays the mind of a young woman of our own time, temporarily imprisoned in the gross body of one of the caste of Mothers. The core of the story, occupying one-third of its length, is a conversation between Jane, the transplanted girl, and Laura, an elderly historian. The dialogue between the opponent of some new order and its champion is a staple manoeuvre of science fiction, from *Brave New World* to the Winston-O'Brien conversations of *Nineteen Eighty-Four* and parts of Bradbury's *Fahrenheit 451*, which we shall be dealing with later. As is usual, Laura is not only a thoughtful and intelligent person but gets the best of the argument, saying all that can be said for the notion that women would be better off without men and making what seem to me some fairly damaging criticisms of the contemporary female role:

"At the beginning of the twentieth century women were starting to have their chance to lead useful, creative, interesting lives. But that did not suit commerce: it needed them much more as mass-consumers than as producers—except on the most routine levels. So Romance was adopted and developed as a weapon against their further progress and to promote consumption, and it was used intensively. Women must never for a moment be allowed to forget their sex, and compete as equals. Everything had to have a 'feminine angle' which must be different from the masculine angle, and be dinned in without ceasing. It would have been unpopular for manufacturers actually to issue an order 'back to the kitchen,' but there were other ways. A profession without a difference, called 'housewife,' could be invented. . . .

"You see, the great hopes for the emancipation of women with which the century had started had been outflanked. Purchasing-power had passed into the hands of the ill-educated and highly suggestible. The desire for Romance is essentially a selfish wish, and when it is encouraged to dominate every other it breaks down all corporate loyalties. The individual woman thus separated from, and yet at the same time thrust into competition with, all other women was almost defenceless; she became . . . in a new, a subtler way, more exploited, more dependent, and less creative than she had ever been before."

So says Laura, and much more. Now I am not claiming either profundity or originality for these utterances of hers, although I do think that in these regards, and in that of ordinary literacy, they have nothing to fear from a comparison with most cultural diagnostics. What I want to emphasize is the fact, rather novel at first glance, that the author is a regular science-fiction writer, well known to readers of *Astounding* and *Amazing* who will certainly not, I am prepared to bet, regard "Consider Her Ways" as an unwarrantable excursion into the dialectic and away from the true path of BEMs and stellar federations. Such toughness on the part of a pulp-magazine audience is encouraging and—when one imagines how a reader of Westerns would take to a twenty-page discussion of frontier ethics— singular. In conclusion, this story would not be science fiction if it failed to leave in the mind some slight discomfort, corresponding perhaps to the purgative effects attributed to tragedy. In the present case, this feeling is indeed slight, being based on nothing more than uneasiness about experiments with viruses; with *World Without Men*, it may be slightly more than slight. It appears that while the manuscript was in the publisher's hands, two reports appeared in the press, one about successful research on an oral contraceptive, the other about successful experiments producing parthenogenesis in turkeys. I think these two prospects are of unequal attractiveness.

There follows a substantial leap in a new direction, undertaken because another reasonably self-contained topic lies at the far end of it. This is the problem of colonialism. As I have already shown, science fiction is full of conventions, from the space-warp to the celebrated Three Laws of Robotics. An equally prominent one says that while an interplanetary expedition can do more or less as it likes with any merely animal forms of life encountered, it must not interfere with alien intelligence—except in self-defence, of course. I still patiently await a story putting forward the immoderately liberal view that the inhabitants of Procyon IX would be perfectly justified in resisting the arrival of Earthmen, even to the point of engulfing them. The right of the explorers—naturally they will be American or British explorers—to go round setting up their trading stations wherever they please is similarly taken for granted in science fiction, as such things are in many other circles. However: the concept of dealing kindly with the intelligent, while setting off a good deal of naïve speculation about the difficulty of measuring the IQ of a Procyonian, is reassuringly widespread, carrying as it does the rider that if their way is not our way (a pretty safe assumption), it must nonetheless be respected. We have already seen this attitude at work in the story called "Big Sword," about the diminutive aliens helped out by a small boy. It reappears in a grimmer form in another biological-puzzle piece, "Unhuman Sacrifice," by an excellent woman writer, Katherine MacLean. Here we meet an alien nation, humanoid in appearance, whose custom it is to hang up all their young people on tree branches, head downward, during the season of floods. Many of them die as a result of this treatment, the reason for which has been forgotten. With that deeply embedded hostility of science-fiction writers to things evangelical, an unstable, canting preacher is introduced, bawling through the translation machine appeals to stop this un-Christian practice. The scientists of the expedition, unwillingly converted to the preacher's view, cut down from his tree a young alien they have befriended and bear him off to presumptive safety through the rising waters. On the way, however, the alien, struggling clear of his helpers,

plunged his hands with spread fingers deep into the mud, and gripped his ankles, as if he had always known just how to do this thing. His hands locked and became unable to unfold. They would never unfold again.

He felt the soft surge that was the first flood wave arriving and passing above him, and ignored it, and, with a mixture of terror and the certainty of doing right, he opened his mouth and took a deep breath of cold water.

All thought stopped. As the water rushed into his lungs, the rooted sea creature that was the forgotten adult stage of [his] species began its thoughtless pseudo-plant existence, forgetting everything that had ever happened to it. Its shape changed.

I take this, not too fancifully I hope, as a justifiably horrifying little allegory of what you can do to people when you interfere with them for their own good, but although I am sure Miss MacLean knew what she was writing, I wonder how many of her readers would have made the extension whereby her point becomes a political one. Still, a satire on organised religion, such as the story patently is, has its own place.

There could be no mistake about what is being said in "The Helping Hand," by Poul Anderson. Of two alien cultures, one accepts the proffered technological aid from

Earth, the other refuses it. The closing scenes show us the independent aliens respected and prosperous, their native culture in fine shape, while those that have received help are miserable second-rate copies of Earthmen, their languages, religion, art, and social customs dying out, sex relations "as casual as on Earth itself," no more tribal farms, no local dishes or handmade pots, "no more bards chanting the old lays and making new ones. They look at the telescreen now." Worst of all, they see themselves as quaint survivals, living off the Earth tourist trade. Just in case we might miss the point, one of the independent aliens harks us back to the twentieth century, when "with the best intentions in the world, the West annihilated all other ways of life."* This story raises a query applying to many, that since its theme is a manifestly contemporary one, would it not be better in contemporary dress? Perhaps, but quite apart from the disagreeable amount of research involved, one might be hard put to avoid unwanted local associations, to excise all accidentals and not be left with something as abstract as a couple of fictitious planets; better to go straight to the generalising medium. Further, a speculative story simply has more chance of getting published if it is science fiction; there are cases on record of writers having to kit out contemporary narratives with aliens and spaceships in order to make a sale. This perhaps says little for the merit of these stories in either form, but it says no more for the enterprise of conventional magazine outlets.

Another leap, squarely into the immense field of science-fiction politics, cannot long be delayed. Here the note of

* Those interested in the notion that the American psyche is tormented by guilt over the subjugation of the Indians would find much useful material in science fiction. Apart from such possible allegories as the Anderson story, there are plenty of specific references, and popular and resourceful Amerinds turn up in the space services with a frequency out of all proportion to the present numbers of that people.

scepticism, of the need to be swimming against the stream, is clearly and repeatedly sounded. In particular, the social value of the deviate, the maverick, is canvassed at all levels of sophistication. Not for nothing is the unsociable, pipe-smoking physicist (he of the beautiful daughter, the solitary devoted assistant who thinks of him as the Old Man, and the jealous bureaucratic band of colleagues) one who has become an archetype. A footnote to William Whyte, "The Organisation Man in Science Fiction," is waiting to be written. It will be a short footnote, for the one has very little to do with the other. If Commander Queeg of the U.S.S. *Caine* had held his commission from the space navy, nobody would have been found to defend him. Scientism, the belief that any day now someone will discover a way of measuring human personality and society, is admittedly rather widespread in science fiction, but there is almost no trace of the tendency to rate the interests of the group higher than those of the individual. A story by Clifford Simak, "Drop Dead," tells how a party of explorers with no food left decide to eat an outlandish-looking, but palatable, creature that lives round about in great numbers, discovering too late that whoever eats a creature ends by turning into a creature. The ulcerated member of the team, who has plenty of his own special food left, throws in his lot with the group by eating a creature himself, and not out of fear of loneliness or attack, but simply as a gesture of solidarity. But such frenzies of the corporate spirit are rare. On a more mundane level, the only pro-group story I can recall is Robert Heinlein's "Coventry," in which the potential deviate's already extremist occupation is that of literary critic. Coventry, an undefined area somewhere on the Canadian border, contains three societies, one corrupt-capitalist, one totalitarian, and one (inevitably) evangelical. The ex-critic decides that even the conformist U.S.A. is better and

returns to join its secret service, a group-solidarity move if
you like, but the story is more than anything else a satire
on ridiculously rugged individualism and the dependence
of even the least pampered upon machines and the creature
comforts they provide.

Convinced assertions of the value of the deviate are
abundant and varied. A favourite stratagem emphasises the
point by making the deviate a repellent person, devoid of
even the least arguable social graces. One such is Rafferty
in Frederik Pohl's "Rafferty's Reasons," a psychotic ex-
artist whose reasons for killing his boss are bad because
eccentric and egotistical, and yet good because eccentric
and viewable as a protest against a society in which voluntary unemployment is a crime, and leisure, unlike what
it is in most utopias, is only available to the powerful. A
more extreme case is the protagonist of "The Country of
the Kind," by Damon Knight, a practising artist this time,
apparently the only one left in a world built on universal
benevolence and unbreakable social graciousness, a world
that is hellish because without conflict. The artist, when
not engaged on impromptu sculpture, goes round breaking
into people's houses and pouring hot soup over their furniture, a gesture again unjustified and justified. By a nice
symbolical touch, he has been operated on at the authori-
ties' direction and given an intolerable smell which cuts
him off from all human intercourse. Some readers will not
be able to avoid seeing in all this a comparatively sober
account of the behaviour of their own arty friends, but the
importance of the sculptor's final message and the clarity
of its relation to all manner of recent and contemporary
non-science-fiction writing are obvious:

YOU CAN SHARE THE WORLD WITH ME. THEY CAN'T STOP YOU.
STRIKE NOW—PICK UP A SHARP THING AND STAB, OR A HEAVY

THING AND CRUSH. THAT'S ALL. THAT WILL MAKE YOU FREE. ANYONE CAN DO IT.

Some writers will take the argument further than this, and produce via atomic radiation and its consequences what is in effect a new type of human being, sometimes outré in appearance, more often gifted with the "wild talent" which has become a science-fiction catch-phrase and convention. By an overwhelming vote, the talent is going to be—and here I could feel quite complacently sceptical were it not for what I reported in an earlier section, the interest taken by Westinghouse—extrasensory perception, perhaps with the decorative additions of telekinesis (moving objects about by the power of the mind) and teleportation (moving yourself about). The picture of a telepathic or psionic or esper or peeper aristocracy given in *The Demolished Man* is comparatively uncommon: much more often we are shown the first telepaths being relentlessly hunted down by the non-gifted mass of humanity, and it is hard not to see in this an allegory of intolerant conformism, especially since the authors are given to explaining that it is just that. Recently I have detected a drift away from psi, no doubt in belated recognition that the available plots are few, and tedious play with mind blocks and thought screens is involved; a funny or satirical mind block, like the unforgettably banal tune in *The Demolished Man*, is rare. I might just add as a sociological note that the editor of *Astounding*, himself a deviant figure of marked ferocity, seems to think he has invented a psi machine, but its nature and purpose I cannot discover.

Conformist utopias maintained by deliberate political effort are a cherished nightmare of contemporary science fiction, and as so often it is by the feebler and less original work that one can gauge the firmness with which the idea has taken hold. Whereas twenty years ago the average yawn-enforcer would locate its authoritarian society on Venus or in the thirtieth century, it would nowadays, I think, set its sights at Earth within the next hundred years or so. The machinery of oppression, again, is wielded not by decadent quasi-aristocrats in ceremonial dress—these are far more common in fantasy—but by businesslike managerial types well equipped with the latest technological and psychological techniques for the prevention or detection of heresy. Thus an incomparably wearisome story I once read—on a train, let it be noted—postulated a synthetic being called the Superfather, who exceeded Orwell's Big Brother in deviousness by persuading you to go and tell him your troubles, a course found to be inadvisable. *Nineteen Eighty-Four* itself, of course, that great work of private hysteria, is a well-known example of the malevolently totalitarian utopia; also abundant are those founded on mistaken notions of benevolence. The October *Fantastic Universe* carried a story called "Let the Dream Die," which rehearsed with plodding exactitude the established anti-conformist arguments of the category, giving off a tinny echo of the conversations between Huxley's two mouthpieces in its final scene. This takes place, typically enough, after the freedom party have successfully attacked their overlords. To the accusation that "strife and rivalry and fear and hatred" will thus be brought back into the world, the leader of the revolutionaries replies:

"Man must take chances with his own follies. Nobody can save him from himself. . . . Man was not meant to dream away his life in slavery, in drugged and hypnotised stupor. Peace is wonderful, but not at the price of living death. We must take our chances as a thinking and deciding animal. . . . We have to make our own choices or we cease to exist as men."

A lighter and less dedicated tone than that, fortunately, is to be found in some other stories under this heading, William Tenn's "Null-P" for instance. Addicts will take the title as a jesting by-blow at A. E. van Vogt's wild and whirling utopia, *The World of Null-A* and its sequel. The A in that case is Aristotle and his logic, and one expects much from a Korzybskian society that denies him, with a couple of null-Es, Euclid and Einstein, thrown in for good measure, but van Vogt is discreditably reticent when it comes to embodying these ideas. In any event, the Tenn story is direct enough: the P is Plato and the notions stemming from him about the importance of merit as a qualification for political leadership. In a world of mounting divergences—an atomic war has produced an enormous harvest of mutations—the American electorate send to the White House a man called George Abnego, the only man in the country who incarnates the statistical average down to the condition and quantity of the very teeth in his mouth: "the median made flesh," as one character puts it. Mediocrity, once enthroned, becomes systematic; authority is in the hands of the non-élite, or unbest, and the only measure ever approved by World President Abnego I— President Abnego VI of the United States—is that "granting preferential university scholarship to students who were closest to their age-group median all over the planet." Eventually, *homo abnegus* is domesticated by a race of intelligent Newfoundland retrievers, who prize him for his stick-throwing abilities and initiate selective breeding to this end. With the development of a machine that can throw sticks farther and quicker, man disappears, "except in the most backward canine communities." The tale is written with a sprightliness and an obvious delight in invention that typifies much of the best contemporary science fiction, which as a whole shows a far wider variety of mood than

superficial inspection reveals. With any story that presents
a recognisable future, one may be hard put to it to distinguish satire from warning, but in this case one would be
safe, I take it, in concluding that the satirical element pre-
dominates. What is conspicuously missing from "Null-P"
is any allusion to existing personalities along the lines of
traditional political satire, a deficiency universal in science
fiction. I grant that I might miss American references in
an individual story, but not in all such; further, in the
present self-examining and self-congratulating phase of the
medium, a claim to have inherited the mantle of Pope or
Swift would certainly have been advanced if it had the
minutest justification. Nor is this lack the sinister index of
some fresh American debility: the British writers don't
satirise individuals either, and in my patriotic way I feel
that any count of personalities ripe for treatment in some
grisly utopia would put Britain firmly in the lead. I cannot
feel that this unwillingness to wound springs from any
deficiencies in the medium itself, and I hope I am not
being merely romantic when I look to the near future for
science fiction that moves on from satirising politicians and
corporations to really spiteful attacks on politician A and
corporation B. In spite of all the talk, the role of science
fiction as an educative force is still gravely undervalued.

The political morals implied by the generic science-fiction utopia are above reproach if one happens to like
democracy. Express or tacit approval of authoritarianism, of
any régime built on gross inequality or the suppression of
freedom, of any state of society that licenses cruelty or
irresponsible whim—these belong to the domain of fantasy.
An extreme, but instructive, example is afforded by the
work of one Sarban, who I should guess to be an established
British writer preferring on occasion to become pseudony-
mous. This self-effacement is understandable on a reading

of his novel *The Sound of His Horn.* Here we presuppose
a Nazi victory in World War II and the installation of a
kind of feudalism whereby the barons and their friends
have a wonderful time riding out of their lodges and enjoying a day's hunting, the quarry normally consisting of
peasants on foot, but on special occasions young ladies
fetichistically arrayed. What Sarban is obviously up to is
writing out his fantasy in another sense of the word, and
doing it in prose of greater energy and power than almost
any science-fiction writer can command, so much so that
I have never been able since to feel quite the same about
the innocent hunting song from which the title is taken. I
need hardly add at this stage of the game that a science-
fiction story on this theme, apart from starting out with
some double-talk about a parallel time-stream to take care
of that Nazi victory, would have got some guns into the
hands of those peasants by about two-thirds of the way
through and would have wrapped up the young ladies in
veils of abstractions and outraged modesty. I am not saying, by the way, that fantasy often embodies Sarban's kind
of fantasy, only that science fiction never does, or only does,
as in Alfred Bester's "The Starcomber," as material for a
critique.

A régime like that visualised by Sarban would not, of
course, be liable to interest a science-fiction writer, whose
hells are always urban. Some of these seem to lie round
the next corner or so, the age of the air-raid shelter, for
example, as in James Blish's *A Case of Conscience,* with the
New York Target Area Authority keeping everyone living
underground and, as a matter of course, hugely psychotic.
More often, though, especially if induced conformity is
coming under fire, something more remote and metaphori-
cal is preferred. In Anthony Boucher's "Barrier" we encounter a society which has defined itself as perfect in all

ways, so that the notion of change becomes blasphemous:
the state's duty is to maintain the Stasis of Cosmos. The
embodiments of this vary from the adjustment or cretinisa-
tion of deviates to the prohibition in music of changes of
key or time. Boucher's best invention here is a special
language in which all irregularity is prohibited and the
articles are dropped as unnecessary and misleading:

". . . they prohibited all drinking because drinking makes you
think world bees better than it really bees and of course if you
make yourself different world that bees against Stasis and so
they prohibited it but they kept on using it for medical purposes and that beed in warehouses and pretty soon no one
knowed any other kind of liquor so it bees called bond."

The linguistic reforms exemplified here derive from a work
called *This Bees Speech*, which, as fictional books go,
sounds rather nicer than, say, *The Complete Poems of
Jeffrey Aspern*. "Barrier" and Tenn's "Null-P" are instances of the comic-inferno type of science fiction to which
I shall be reverting later. For a moment, I want to pursue
the notion of political conformism in its more earnest forms,
doing no more than mention a story in which the major
act of the oppressive government is the banning of science
fiction, whereupon the fan clubs become proscribed revolutionary organisations.

A very representative story, though written with unusual
conviction, is Robert Sheckley's "The Academy." Here the
detection of deviates is achieved by the use of nasty machines called sanity meters with scales calibrated from zero
to ten. Whenever you pass near one of these things—and
every public place has one—the needle indicates your
sanity rating. "The normalcy range for our civilisation lies
between zero and three"; above seven you become unsane
and on reaching ten you forfeit your citizenship and "must

undergo surgical alteration or may submit voluntarily to therapy at The Academy." Thus is preserved the so-called Status Quo, corresponding to the Stasis in Boucher's story. The hero, Feerman, naturally finds himself in due course at The Academy, an institution whose record of cures is a hundred per cent, but from which no one is ever discharged. The doctor there, more humane than Orwell's O'Brien and less loquacious than Huxley's Mond, explains to Feerman that "movement in any direction harms a static society," which "must be protected against the individual." An injection is administered. What follows I will quote at some length:

When he recovered consciousness he found that he was standing on a great plain. It was sunrise. In the dim light, wisps of fog clung to his ankles, and the grass beneath his feet was wet and springy.

Feerman was mildly surprised to see his wife standing beside him, close to his right side. On his left was his dog Speed, pressed against his leg, trembling slightly. His surprise passed quickly, because this was where his wife and dog should be, at his side before the battle.

Ahead, misty movement resolved into individual figures, and as they approached Feerman recognised them.

They were the enemy! Leading the procession was his robutler, gleaming inhumanly in the half-light. Morgan [his boss] was there, shrieking to the Section Chief that Feerman must die. . . . And there was his landlady, screaming, "No home for him!" and behind her were doctors, receptionists, guards and behind them marched millions of men in rough laborer's clothing, caps jammed down over their faces, newspapers tightly rolled as they advanced.

Feerman tensed expectantly for this ultimate fight against the enemies who had betrayed him. But a doubt passed over his mind. Was this real?

He had a sudden sickening vision of his drugged body lying

in a numbered room in The Academy, while his soul was here in the never-never land, doing battle with shadows.

There's nothing wrong with me! In a moment of utter clarity, Feerman understood that he had to escape. . . . He had to get back to the real world. The Status Quo couldn't last for ever. And what would mankind do, with all the toughness, inventiveness, individuality bred out of the race?

Did no one leave the Academy? He would! Feerman struggled with the illusions, and he could almost feel his discarded body stir on its couch, groan, move. . . .

But his dream-wife seized his arm and pointed. His dream-dog snarled at the advancing host.

The moment was gone forever, but Feerman never knew it. He forgot his decision, forgot earth, forgot truth, and drops of dew spattered his legs as he ran forward to engage the enemy in battle.

Such modest power as this extract possesses derives, I suppose, from the fact that it allegorises at least two cultural factors: the diversion of creative energy into channels that are not serious, and so both harmless and useless; and secondly, the organisation man's view that protest, if not the mark of a sanity reading in motion away from the norm, is a wish-fulfilling battle against shadows. From what I know of Sheckley's work, I should say that he is quite clever enough to have known what he was doing, and it hardly matters if he didn't, because, as we all know, a writer's view of what he was doing is no more valid than anyone else's.

Finally, I want to examine with similar intensity two pieces by Ray Bradbury, a short story and a short novel. Bradbury is the Louis Armstrong of science fiction, not in the sense of age or self-repetition but in that he is the one practitioner well known by name to those who know nothing whatever about his field. How this has happened

I am not quite sure; perhaps it was that early pat on the head he got from Christopher Isherwood; perhaps it is his tendency to fall into that particular kind of sub-whimsical, would-be poetical badness that goes straight to the corny old heart of the Sunday reviewer:

Martin knew it was autumn again, for Dog ran into the house bringing wind and frost and a smell of apples turned to cider under trees. In dark clock-springs of hair, Dog fetched golden-rod, dust of farewell-summer, acorn-husk, hair of squirrel, feather of departed robin, sawdust from fresh-cut cordwood, and leaves like charcoals shaken from a blaze of maple-trees. Dog jumped. Showers of brittle fern, blackberry vine, marsh-grass sprang over the bed where Martin shouted. No doubt, no doubt of it at all, this incredible beast was October!

Such a poem in October would certainly appeal to the author of *This Bees Speech*, whose view it was that "article bees prime corruptor of human thinking." Another and much more unlikely reason for Bradbury's fame is that, despite his regrettable tendency to dime-a-dozen sensitivity, he is a good writer, wider in range than any of his colleagues, capable of seeing life on another planet as something extraordinary instead of just challenging or horrific, ready to combine this with strongly held convictions. These last, at any rate, appear in his story "Usher II," which opens on Mars with the building of a residence after the prescription in Poe's story, great care having been taken to get the tarn "black and lurid" enough, the sedge satisfactorily "gray and ebon," etc. Inside, there are copper bats controlled by electronic beams, brass rats, robot skeletons, and phantoms. Soon the Investigator of Moral Climates, one Garrett, arrives and orders demolition, under the ordinances which have prohibited and destroyed all works of fantasy from Poe to *The Wizard of Oz*, while no films

are allowed except remakes of Ernest Hemingway. There is
time for one huge party, at which all the guests are members of the Society for the Prevention of Fantasy and are
publicly murdered one after another by robot apes, bi-
sected by pendulums, prematurely buried, and so on. Garrett himself is led into the catacombs by Stendahl, the
owner, who mentions Amontillado and produces a mason's
trowel without drawing any reaction from Garrett. The
rest is soon told:

"Garrett," said Stendahl, "do you know why I've done this to
you? Because you burned Mr. Poe's books without really reading them. You took other people's advice that they needed
burning. Otherwise you'd have realised what I was going to
do to you when we came down here a moment ago. Ignorance
is fatal, Mr. Garrett."

Garrett was silent.

"I want this to be perfect," said Stendahl, holding his lantern
so its light penetrated in upon the slumped figure. "Jingle your
bells softly." The bells rustled. "Now, if you'll please say, 'For
the love of God, Montresor,' I might let you free."

The man's face came up in the light. There was a hesitation.
Then grotesquely the man said, "For the love of God, Montresor."

"Ah," said Stendahl, eyes closed. He shoved the last brick
into place and mortared it tight. "*Requiescat in pace*, dear
friend."

He hastened from the catacomb.

The suppression of fantasy, or of all books, is an aspect of
the conformist society often mentioned by other writers,
but with Bradbury it is a specialty. His novel *Fahrenheit
451*—supposedly the temperature at which book-paper ig-
nites—extends and fills in the assumptions of "Usher II."
The hero, Montag, is a fireman, which means that on receiving an alarm he and his colleagues pile on to the wagon

and go off and burn somebody's house down, one with books in it, under the regulations of the Firemen of America, "established, 1790, to burn English-influenced books in the Colonies. First Fireman: Benjamin Franklin." In the expected central dialogue, the fire chief explains to Montag how it all came about:

"Classics cut to fit fifteen-minute radio shows, then cut again to fill a two-minute book column, winding up at last as a ten- or twelve-line dictionary resume. I exaggerate, of course. The dictionaries were for reference. But many were those whose sole knowledge of *Hamlet* . . . was a one-page digest in a book that claimed: *now at last you can read all the classics; keep up with your neighbors.* Do you see? Out of the nursery into the college and back to the nursery; there's your intellectual pattern. . . . Life is immediate, the job counts, pleasure lies all about after work. . . . More sports for everyone, group spirit, fun, and you don't have to think, eh? . . . Authors, full of evil thoughts, lock up your typewriters. . . . We must be all alike. Not everyone born free and equal, as the Constitution says, but everyone *made* equal. Each man the image of every other; then all are happy, for there are no mountains to make them cower, to judge themselves against. So! A book is a loaded gun in the house next door. Burn it. Take the shot from the weapon. . . . Ask yourself, What do we want in this country above all? People want to be happy, isn't that right? Haven't you heard it all your life? I want to be happy, people say. Well, aren't they? Don't we keep them moving, don't we give them fun? That's all we live for, isn't it? For pleasure, for titillation? And you must admit our culture provides plenty of these. . . . If you don't want a man unhappy politically, don't give him two sides to a question to worry him; give him one. Better yet, give him none. . . . Don't give [him] any slippery stuff like philosophy or sociology to tie things up with. That way lies melancholy."

One could offer plenty of objections to that, starting with the apparently small point that complacency about sociology, which Bradbury shares with his colleagues, is at least as bad as complacency about the tabloidisation of the classics, and that what we ought to want is less sociology, not more. Further, there is about Bradbury, as about those I might call the non-fiction holders of his point of view, a certain triumphant lugubriousness, a kind of proleptic *schadenfreude* (world copyright reserved), a relish not always distinguishable here from satisfaction in urging a case, but different from it, and recalling the relish with which are recounted the horrors of *Nineteen Eighty-Four* and a famous passage that prefigures it in *Coming Up for Air*. Jeremiah has never had much success in pretending he doesn't thoroughly enjoy his job, and whereas I agree with him, on the whole, in his dislike of those who reach for their revolver when they hear the word "culture," I myself am getting to the point where I reach for my ear-plugs on hearing the phrase "decline of our culture." But in this respect Bradbury sins no more grievously than his non-fiction colleagues, whom he certainly surpasses in immediacy, for *Fahrenheit 451* is a fast and scaring narrative, a virtue hard to illustrate by quotation. There are at least two good dramatic coups, one when a creature called the Mechanical Hound, constructed to hunt down book-owners and other heretics, looks up from its kennel in the fire station and growls at the hero, the other when Montag goes out on duty with the Salamander, as the fire engine is called, and finds that the alarm refers to his own house. The book emerges quite creditably from a comparison with *Nineteen Eighty-Four* as inferior in power, but superior in conciseness and objectivity. At the end, of course, Montag eludes the Mechanical Hound and joins a band of distinguished hoboes who are preserving the classics by learning them by heart.

Bradbury's is the most skilfully drawn of all science

fiction's conformist hells. One invariable feature of them is that however activist they may be, however convinced that the individual can, and will, assert himself, their programme is always to resist or undo harmful change, not to promote useful change. It is quite typical that the revolutionary party in *The Space Merchants* should be called the Conservationists. Thus to call the generic political stance of science fiction "radical," as I have done, is not quite precise: it is radical in attitude and temper, but strongly conservative in alignment.* This, however, does not weaken its claim to be regarded as, some of the time and in some sense, a literature of warning, as propaganda, not always unintelligent, against the notion that we can leave the experts to work things out for us. Such is equally the impression given, I think, by our next topic, utopias in which the forces of evil show themselves in economic and technological, rather than political, terms. As I said at the beginning, these departments are not, and should not be, readily separable, but emphasis can be graded. In the next section I shall show how Mrs. Montag amused herself while Montag was busy on his incendiary routine of "Monday . . . Millay, Wednesday Whitman, Friday Faulkner."

---

* "Negative" might be a better description. Such glimpses of the post-totalitarian future as we can glean show a society just like our own, but with more decency and less television. Nobody ever says how these reforms are to be brought about. Further, no positive utopias, dramatising schemes of political or other betterment, can be found in contemporary science fiction. Modern visionaries in general seem to have lost interest in any kind of social change, falling back on notions of self-salvation via naturopathy, orgonomy, or the psychic diagnostics of Edgar Cayce.

Without turning on the light he imagined how this room would look. His wife stretched on the bed, uncovered and cold, like a body displayed on the lid of a tomb, her eyes fixed to the ceiling by invisible threads of steel, immovable. And in her ears the little Seashells, the thimble radios tamped tight, and an electronic ocean of sound, of music and talk and music and talk coming in, coming in on the shore of her unsleeping mind. The room was indeed empty. Every night the waves came in and bore her off on their great tides of sound, floating her, wide-eyed, toward morning. There had been no night in the last two years that Mildred had not swum that sea, had not gladly gone down in it for the third time.

As regular readers will have guessed, Mildred is Mrs. Montag, wife of Ray Bradbury's book-burning fireman. It emerges, I think, that while it will not do for science fiction to characterize in conventional, differentiating terms, it can have something to say about human nature by dint of isolating and extending some observable tendency of behaviour, by showing, in this case, how far the devolution of individuality might go if the environment were to be modified in a direction favourable to this devolution. The lesson to be drawn from the more imaginative science-fiction hells, such as Bradbury's, is not only that a society could be devised that would frustrate the active virtues,

111

nor even that these could eventually be suppressed, but that there is in all sorts of people something that longs for this to happen. There are plenty of embryonic Mrs. Montags waiting for the chance to be wafted away by the Seashells,* or to share her jolly evenings at the Fun Park, breaking windows or smashing up cars with the steel ball, to join with her in watching three-wall television and trying to persuade her husband to get the fourth wall put in. This eager denial of mind, this longing to abandon reality via mechanical wonders, is obviously relevant to the political thesis of Bradbury's *Fahrenheit 451* and of many other works: the deliberate use of technology to promote an unworthy quiescence is a familiar idea. Correspondingly, Mildred Montag is a victim of epidemic neurosis: a cleverly staged scene shows her being brought round after a suicide attempt by a couple of cigarette-puffing handymen who just have time to use the almost fully automatic evacuation machine on her before rushing off to the next of their dozen nightly cases. What is most important here, however, is clearly the notion of the Seashell jag, for this need presuppose no kind of political manipulation, whether malevolent or mistakenly paternalistic.

Versions of the Seashells occur in the work of many writers primarily concerned to question unrestricted technological and commercial development. Often a novelty is

---

* Bradbury himself notes:

In writing the short novel "Fahrenheit 451," I thought I was describing a world that might evolve in four or five decades. But only a few weeks ago, in Beverly Hills one night, a husband and wife passed me, walking their dog. I stood staring after them, absolutely stunned. The woman held in one hand a small cigarette-package-sized radio, its antenna quivering. From this sprang tiny copper wires which ended in a dainty cone plugged into her right ear. There she was, oblivious to man and dog, listening to far winds and whispers and soap-opera cries, sleepwalking, helped up and down curbs by a husband who might just as well not have been there. This was not *fiction.*

envisaged which is not only more pleasurable than that reality which Mr. Eliot says we cannot bear very much of, but also as durable. There is actually no reason why Mildred Montag should ever have done anything else but listen to the Seashells, an idea taken to its logical conclusion in a delightfully nasty little story by John D. MacDonald, "Spectator Sport." A man who has been given a pre-frontal lobotomy by mistake is compensated by receiving for nothing what everybody else is saving up all his money for: total and irrevocable immersion in three-dimensional panaesthetic participatory television, the favourite series opted for being Western, Crime and Detection, and Harem. A pair of bored technicians, first cousins to Bradbury's anti-suicide team, are hurrying around doing the requisite surgery on the day's quota. A variation on this theme takes the form of an admonitory satire on tranquillisers in Frederik Pohl's story "What To Do Till the Analyst Comes." After an unusually severe lung-cancer scare, the researchers come up with a chewing gum containing a euphoric drug that is not addictive, simply very agreeable. The whole world takes up Cheery-Gum, becoming totally happy and unneurotic and idle, secure in the knowledge that the stuff can be given up at any time, just as bridge-playing can. Only the hero is prevented by an allergy from joining in the universal merry-go-round.

Despite its lighthearted tone, what is at work in this story is obviously the same as that in "Spectator Sport" and Bradbury's Seashell episode: the fear of a pleasure so overmastering that it can break down the sense of reality or at least the pattern of active life, and break them down in everyone, not merely in the predisposed neurotic. This feeling is not always treated thematically; it appears significantly often as background decoration, and I might almost have fitted it into my discussion of science fiction and the unconscious, were it not so conscious. In the preface to a collection containing one such story—the agent here is a melody, mathematically arrived at of course, which produces catatonic ecstasy—Arthur Clarke notes an article in the *Scientific American* for October, 1956; the subject: "Pleasure Centers in the Brain." It seems that the electrical stimulation of a certain part of a rat's brain causes the animal intense pleasure. When the rat finds it can stimulate itself for a second or so by pressing a lever, it spends most of its time doing this.

Electric stimulation in some of these regions actually appeared to be far more rewarding to the animals than an ordinary satisfier such as food. For example, hungry rats ran faster to reach an electric stimulator than they did to reach food. Indeed, a hungry animal often ignored available food in favor of the pleasure of stimulating itself electrically. Some rats . . . stimulated their brains more than 2,000 times per hour for 24 consecutive hours! . . . Enough of the brain-stimulating work has been repeated on monkeys . . . to indicate that our general conclusions can very likely be generalised eventually to human beings—with modifications, of course.

I cannot say that I feel more frightened by that than by any crisis in Berlin or around Formosa, but I think perhaps I should.

It is remarkable, as I have nearly or possibly quite said before, how rarely the sinister developments foreseen include sex. Amid the most elaborate technological innovations, the most *outré* political or economic shifts, involving changes in the general conduct of life as extreme as the gulf dividing us from the Middle Ages, man and woman, husband and wife, lover and mistress go on doing their stuff in the mid-twentieth-century way with a kind of brutish imperturbability—assuming that the full biological complement of sexes is maintained. The sentimental consensus that this is perhaps the only part of human nature that can never be changed, unless indeed life itself becomes something else, is a disappointing trait in science-fiction writers, who as a rule are almost over-excitable in their readiness to see as variables what are normally taken to be constants. Accordingly, if a robot wife is introduced, it will be as a means to the conclusion that in one way or another she is not so satisfactory as a human one; if a consignment of girls is sent to mitigate the rigours of the all-male explorers' society on Procyon IX, we can expect to learn that women may cause a whole lot of trouble, but that as against this, they do you good. Gradations of sexual privilege, compulsory chastity plus artificial insemination, demolition for adulterers—I look in vain even for such simplicities as these, all of which strike me as a good deal more plausible than the average alien invasion. The nearest approach to sexual novelty is provided by episodes like the one in *Search the Sky* (Pohl and Kornbluth), where men and women have exchanged roles; the resultant clowning is fun, if rather sedate fun, and there is satire too—opposition to the career-boy is just old-fashioned prejudice, says the female tycoon. But the notion of a feminised society is a mere jumping-off point for comic invention: the authors do not hold it up as a serious possibility or analogy.

Though it may go against the grain to admit it, science-fiction writers are evidently satisfied with the sexual status quo—the female-emancipationism of a Wylie or a Wyndham is too uncommon to be significant. Nor has anything more surprising than a new contraceptive been imagined as a specific pressure operating against that status quo. This is not to say that sexual relations are not often shown as becoming degraded (*i.e.*, promiscuous or venal: the range of degradation envisioned is small); but such matters are regularly taken as a symptom or a part of some larger degradation, political, social, ethical. If sex is elevated, we are shown this as accompanying a larger elevation. Only Robert Sheckley, science fiction's premier gadfly, is capable of imagining an independent sexual revolution: in "A Ticket to Tranai," wives are put into stasis, or suspended animation, when not needed by their husbands, age one year for every dozen on the calendar, and thus enjoy a long succession of married lives, plus the financial benefits of multiple widowhood. The ethics are that you must take your wife out of stasis for at least a few hours a week; the drama comes when the hero won't put his wife in. "Pilgrimage to Earth" introduces a concern called Love, Inc., which provides young ladies specially conditioned to fall in love genuinely, not just as pretence, with any given customer. "If we were selling simulated love," the executive explains to the hero, "we'd label it as such. The advertising laws on Earth are strict, I can assure you. Anything can be sold, but it must be labelled properly. That's ethics!" This prospect seems to outdo the contraption in Arthur Clarke's "Patent Pending," whereby the entirety of a sexual experience can be recorded and played back. In general, it is in terms of violence, rather than of sex in the straightforward sense, that the science-fiction writer will render specific the theme of moral collapse. A representative instance is Pohl and Kornbluth's *Gladiator-at-Law*, which introduces, in the first place, lethal public combats with blowtorch comedy numbers and tightrope walks over a huge tank full of piranhas. In the second place, there is a system of juvenile gang-warfare (outside the arena) with live ammunition and broken bottles. Homicidal children are an immensely popular subject, one of the very few appearing with similar frequency in both science fiction and fantasy; one would place in the latter field, I suppose, Ray Bradbury's Small Assassin, who disposes of both his parents at the age of three months. The most horrifying modern fantasy story I have ever read, Jerome Bixby's "It's a *Good Life*," centres on a three-year-old child who is literally omnipotent. On the grown-up level, several writers devise a socially approved system of murder committed as therapy for the murderer or simply for fun, and the correlation between a regularised society and the incidence of uncontrollable destructive urges is even more widely explored. Often our own time will be treated as a kind of Capone-period Chicago to which refugee violence-addicts from a humanitarian future will travel in order to go on the rampage.

Imaginings about violence provide many of science fiction's most pessimistic moments, but they need not be so used. An often-overlooked feature of the medium, and a valuable counterpoise to the heavily moralising tone it sometimes adopts, is its fondness for levity in situations not wholly appropriate to it, which is hopeful, for does not bad taste indicate maturity? Sheckley, though in other ways a serious writer, gives us a variegated comic inferno in the story just mentioned, "A Ticket to Tranai." When not slipping its women in and out of stasis, this anti-conformist society is working off its resentment of machines, particularly robots, and devising better methods of doing so. The hero, a Terran with out-of-date ideas, is eventually persuaded to take a job in the disimprovement branch of the robot works. Here he devises a new, more brittle plastic for the robot's case which will shatter on receiving a kick of more than twenty-three pounds' impact—the research wing have established that this is the average frustration kick. A colleague has disimproved the robot's standard ten-degree list (proved by research to be the most irritating angle) with the aid of a counter-gyroscopic principle and a random selector that makes the robot lurch at unpredictable intervals; the hero finds a way of meshing his own squeak-and-grind unit with the lurch control, and the technical journals are ecstatic. The main object of disimprovement engineering is to increase the customer's rage-level and thus make his destruction of the robot more psychologically valuable to him; as a secondary consideration it furthers the commercial aim of built-in obsolescence. The jesting tone of this story accompanies a delight in consistent and concrete elaboration that typifies the comic inferno and may be its main effect. The suitability of this to satire on aspects of modern consumer-society is obvious, or at least will be repeatedly argued in what is to follow. Such aspects come to the fore in another Sheckley story, "Cost of Living." Here the citizen with the helicopter and the subterranean swimming-pool and other marvels, together with a $200,000 debt, finds that he can have more of both by mortgaging the first thirty years' worth of his son's earnings, and if necessary can do the same for his grandchildren up to their full life-expectancy. About this point the hilarity dims slightly, and vanishes altogether before the end, where we see the man at his job, sitting at the end of an assembly-line pressing buttons on a succession of washing machines to find out if they are all right. They always are.

We have now reached the point of departure for the consideration, in some detail, of the work of Frederik Pohl, the most consistently able writer science fiction, in the modern sense, has yet produced. His field of interest is contemporary urban society and its chain of production and consumption. He is thus in some sort a novelist of economic man, or, rather, of two overlapping personages within that concept, the well-to-do consumer and the high-level executive who keeps the consumer consuming. An occasional space-ship flashes across his page, but no BEM ever raises its heads there and aliens do not appeal to him; the adventure-story component of his work is incidental. His mode is typically the satirical utopia, with comic-inferno elements rarely absent; his method is selective exaggeration of observable features of our society, plus the concrete elaboration noted in Sheckley. These are well illustrated in a story from his aptly named collection *The Case Against Tomorrow*. This story, "The Midas Plague," is a straight comic-inferno satire on the social effects of overproduction. We open with a wedding reception in the quarter-acre, fountain-studded ballroom of the gigantic mansion owned by the hero, Morey Field, complete with its nine special-function robots. The bride's parents, wearing rented garments, eventually drive off in a miniature runabout to their five-room cottage, full of foreboding about the advisability of rich folks marrying poor folks. After a short round of fantastic luxuries, Cherry, the wife, tires even of the expensive companion-robot's anecdotes and bursts into a tearful tirade against the miseries of poverty, for in this society the poor man is he who must consume more than his neighbour. And consumption must be genuine, the Dionysian meals really consumed, the sports gear really worn out in exercise with the sparring-robot, or there will be trouble with the Ration Board, a vast bureaucracy seen as a vigilant nuisance rather than a means of repression, this not being a political satire. Pohl quickly sketches in the domestic and social consequences of

Limitless discovery, infinite power in the atom, tireless labor of humanity and robots, mechanization that drove jungle and swamp and ice off the Earth, and put up office buildings and manufacturing centers in their place. . . .

The pipeline of production spewed out riches that no king in the time of Malthus could have known.

But a pipeline has two ends. The invention and power and

labor pouring in at one end must somehow be drained out at the other. . . .

Lucky Morey, blessed economic-consuming unit, drowning in the pipeline's flood, striving manfully to eat and drink and wear and wear out his share of the ceaseless tide of wealth,

for, as he puts it to himself later, "you can't break eggs without making an omelette." The survey that follows is compact, energetic, inventive, and often comic. I cannot enumerate all the detail, but there is an account of the garishness of slums that cleverly utilises another line of satirical prediction, and a well-devised moment when Morey turns up for his regular psychoanalytic session. It is group therapy, of course, and on this occasion there are eleven in the group: "four Freudians, two Reichians, two Jungians, a Gestalter, a shock therapist and the elderly and rather quiet Sullivanite." Finally Morey brings the two ends of the production pipeline together by arranging for the robots to do all the necessary consuming after being fitted with special satisfaction circuits to obviate the normal legal and moral objections against waste. He moves up to a five-room house, is voted Consumer of the Year, and becomes reconciled with his wife. The Ration Board goes into voluntary liquidation.

I have outlined this story at some length because to do so goes some way to demonstrate the inventive quality I mentioned: once the specific assumption has been set up —one with a satiric value that does no violence to our notions of what is possible—the procedure of the comic inferno is to delineate the social picture by the constant introduction of novelties, these to be, where possible, witty, in the sense that they will strike by their singularity at first sight, but are on reflection found to be just. By "just" I mean that these novelties should extend the original assumption and maintain a corresponding link with the possible; they need show no individual connection with observable features of our own society. The slightest acquaintance shows that to read a science-fiction utopia as one reads the traditional allegory, alert for one-to-one correspondences, is to misread it. If this represents an impoverishment, an unwillingness to face a difficult and more serious task, something may be gained by the resulting liberation of the fancy. If, again, I seem to be justifying a flight from reality and thus from satire, it can be argued that from the good comic inferno, as here, more generalisations than one may emerge. "The Midas Plague" does not merely inform us that the results of over-production may be fantastic, or hilarious, or desperate; it also comments on the revolutions in manners which human beings will swallow—in Morey Field's world you show your politeness by letting the other fellow pick up the restaurant or bar bill—and something too is being said about our adaptability in applying unchanged moral attitudes to changed moral forms—Morey's father-in-law treats a joke about waste with the reluctant abandonment of tolerance with which others might treat a joke about religion. I am not trying to solemnise a *jeu d'esprit*, but considerations like these, along with judgment of the inventive flow, are what enable us to grade science-fiction stories, to decide, for instance, that "The Midas Plague" is superior to another by the same author, "The Wizards of Pung's Corners." Here the techniques of consumer-oriented production are applied to the armoury of the United States forces, with an advertising agency occupying the fifth side of the Pentagon. After some Parkinson's-Law satire on the multiplication of auxiliaries—there are Historical Section tape recorders in every foxhole—the main thrust is reached with the description of the weapons, all of which, naturally, have built-in consumer-dissatisfactions. The 105-mm explosive cannon with Zip-Fire Auto-Load and Wizard-trol Safety Interlock turns out to be no good, the E-Z-Fyre Revolv-a-Clip Carbine is too complicated, and even the "full-color, glossy-paper operating manual—*The Five-Step Magic-Eye Way to New Combat Comfort and Security*" is no help to the troops, who are easily disarmed by a few farmers with shotguns. Though moving at a splendid pace in this scene, invention is rather sparse earlier on, apart from some very funny, but utterly irrelevant, speculation about the selling value of pornographic subliminal commercials on television. Above all, unless I am being unduly optimistic, the initial premise of this story seems too far from plausibility to permit of anything very relevant being said about our own time, and the tendency of soldiers to go on being soldiers even when tinkering with the E-Z-Fyre Carbine is hardly edifying. That rare personage, he who knows something of serious literature and something of science fiction, would conclude that "The Wizards of Pung's Corners" is entertaining but frivolous. But, once more, entertaining; we have not got so much of that in science fiction yet that we can afford to be patronising about it.

So much for the comic inferno, a mode of writing that is clearly older than science fiction, but makes its own humble claim to originality here, in that the absurdities it envisages rest upon conceivable developments in technology: this is an invariable rule. Its moral value, if one must be contrived, is that it ridicules notions which various heavy pressures would have us take seriously: pride in a mounting material standard of living, the belief that such progress can be continued indefinitely and needs only horizontal extension to make the world perfect, the feeling that the accumulation of possessions is at once the prerogative and the evidence of merit. When the science-fiction writer

moves from dealing with the effects of these assumptions
to the forces which manipulate them, his tone will become
notably less jaunty. We have already referred to another
story by Frederik Pohl, "The Tunnel Under the World,"
in which a township is reduced to the status of a human
laboratory for testing sales-reaction. One extra point emerging from it, in the hero's appalled realisation that what
has been done to him and his friends could be done to the
whole world if need be, reflects a widespread anxiety
about the possible political uses of discoveries made in the
commercial field. The fear that some physicist may ac-
cidentally blow the Earth into the sun is evidently being
overhauled by the fear that some researcher working on
consumer resistance will stumble on a subliminal technique
which can be adopted by authority. This is the overt theme
of a dull story called "Take a Deep Breath," where the
success of a hypnotic technique on television induces the
manufacturer to give up making horrible cigarettes and
stand for President. I mention this only because, as before,
the distribution of an idea can best be gauged by its spread
downwards. To return to Frederik Pohl and his tunnel:
the most disturbing part of the story is not so much the
horror-loaded climax as a brief scene in which the con-
trolling power tries out a new advertising procedure. It
starts with a van driving into a residential area playing
at top volume a tape-recording of fire engines answering
an alarm. Then:

The bellow caught him from behind; it was almost like a hard
slap on the ears. A harsh, sneering voice, louder than the
archangel's trumpet, howled:

"Have you got a freezer? *It stinks*! If it isn't a Feckle
Freezer, *it stinks*! If it's a last year's Feckle Freezer, *it stinks*!
Only this year's Feckle Freezer is any good at all! You know
who owns an Ajax Freezer? Fairies own Ajax Freezers! You

know who owns a Triplecold Freezer? Commies own Triplecold Freezers! Every freezer but a brand-new Feckle Freezer *stinks*!"

The voice screamed inarticulately with rage. "I'm warning you! Get out and buy a Feckle Freezer right away! Hurry up! Hurry for Feckle! Hurry, hurry, hurry, Feckle, Feckle, Feckle, Feckle, Feckle, Feckle. . . ."

The effectiveness of that presumably derives not only from the way it dramatises the coercive tendency of some actual advertising, nor from the reflection any of us might have that this is how they would like to talk to us if they dared, but also from its having touched on a truth about the whole advertising idea, that it is an outrage, an assault on people's mental privacy. Here certainly, to my mind, one carries away that residual uneasiness which I mentioned before as the inverted catharsis good science fiction can provide, and which seems to contradict those critics who find in it an oversimplifying complacency posing as moral concern. One would have the best of reasons for disliking the kind of future described in this story, even without reading its entirety as an allegorical account of the thraldom of economic man.

Range of effect is uncommon in science-fiction writers, who show a depressing tendency to re-till their own small plot of ground: one thinks of Clifford Simak with his pastoral pieties, A. E. van Vogt with his superman fantasies, and almost anyone you like (Eric Frank Russell is the least unimaginative example) with his bright adventure stories and incuriosity about human character. Variety that goes beyond mere rearrangement is seldom to be found outside the works of Blish, Bradbury, Clarke, Sheckley, and Pohl, and variety of mood within a single work is rarer still. It does appear, however, in *The Space Merchants*, which has many claims to being the best science-fiction novel so far. It is one of several which Pohl wrote in collaboration with C. M. Kornbluth, a prolific and competent author no longer with us. I will leave to the L. Sprague de Camps of the future the final determination of which partner is responsible for which scenes, but a check of Kornbluth's individual work—*Not This August*, in which America retrieves a total defeat by Russia and China, or *Syndic*, a chronicle of minor wars following upon a major one—soon suggests that his part in *The Space Merchants* was roughly to provide the more violent action while Pohl filled in the social background and the satire. Both sets of interests are appropriate to the construction of a utopia in which the economic system has swallowed the political, with power wielded immediately as well as ultimately by the large companies, the forms of the administration retained for their usefulness as a "clearing house for pressures," and society rigidly stratified into producers, executives, and consumers. The opening is pure Pohl: the hero, Mitchell Courtenay, copy-smith star class, attends a top-level conference of Fowler Schocken Associates, the advertising agency he works for, one of the most puissant and formidable in all Madison Avenue, billing "a mega-buck a year more than anybody else around." The reader is introduced, casually and by degrees, to representative features of the society imagined: the industrial anthro-pology expert reports that while schoolchildren east of the Mississippi are having their lunches—soyaburgers and re-generated steak—packed according to the prescription of a rival firm, their candy, ice cream, and Kiddiebutt ciga-rette ration have been decisively cornered by a Fowler Schocken client, so that the children's future is assured. Similarly, the Coffiest account is mentioned and the cost of the cure from this habit-forming beverage estimated at a nice round five thousand dollars. Finally we come to the Venus project and a preview of the relevant television commercial:

"This is the ship that a modern Columbus will drive through the void," said the voice. "Six and a half million tons of trapped lightning and steel—an ark for eighteen hundred men and women, and everything to make a new world for their home. Who will man it? What fortunate pioneers will tear an empire from the rich, fresh soil of another world? Let me introduce you to them—a man and his wife, two of the intrepid. . . ."

The voice kept on going. On the screen the picture dissolved to a spacious suburban roomette in the early morning. On the screen the husband folding the bed into the wall and taking down the partition to the children's nook; the wife dialing breakfast and erecting the table. Over the breakfast juices and the children's pablum (with a steaming mug of Coffiest for each, of course) they spoke persuasively to each other about how wise and brave they had been to apply for passage in the Venus rocket. And the closing question of their youngest babbler ("Mommy, when I grow up kin I take *my* littul boys and girls to a place as nice as Venus?") cued the switch to a highly imaginative series of shots of Venus as it would be when the child grew up—verdant valleys, crystal lakes, brilliant mountain vistas.

The commentary did not exactly deny, and neither did it dwell on, the decades of hydroponics and life in hermetically sealed cabins that the pioneers would have to endure while working on Venus' unbreathable atmosphere and waterless chemistry.

One can see there the basic ingredients of the method: the detail, the casualness, the use of scattered hints which will cohere as the story progresses. The commercial itself provides that compound of the familiar with the unfamiliar which, as usual, serves the double purpose of inducing the reader to accept an imaginary world while offering him satire on the world he knows, a duality of present and

future which is fundamental to good science fiction and
is here neatly summarised in the title of the novel. Satirical
treatment of the advertising profession as it now is extends
some way into the treatment of character, so that the chief
is a man of huge lyrical complacency, enmeshing all his
subordinates in a web of self-congratulation and gazing
round the conference room "with the air of a day-tripper
in Xanadu"; similarly the Director of Market Research
interrupts to say he just wants "to go on record as agreeing with Mr. Schocken—one hundred per cent—all the
way!" These stock types are handled with wit and imagination, but they are stock types, and it is necessary that they
should be so. In this type of story, which must consistently
stop a good deal short of what is no more than barely
possible, an added reference-point or reassurance to the
reader can be furnished by treating character conservatively
and limiting interest in it; it must be shown quickly that
the familiar categories of human behaviour persist in an
unfamiliar environment, and the book's whole tenor
would be set awry by the kind of specifying, distinguishing,
questioning form of characterisation to which general fiction has accustomed us. A mariner out of Conrad or
Melville would be no use to us in Lilliput or Brobdingnag,
for the point at which specialisation of character becomes
a narrowing and a weakening is reached much sooner in
science fiction than elsewhere. Very often, admittedly, the
merely intrepid space-explorer with his merely sinister and
merely pious companions fatally impoverishes the story
in which he appears, but it is clear, for example, that the girl
Jane in "Consider Her Ways," Wyndham's unisexual
utopia, must not be anything but an averagely sensitive,
averagely romantic young woman of the twentieth century,
with the required above-average score for articulateness;
Morey Field in "The Midas Plague" must be contented,

then bewildered, then ingenious, and nothing more. Science fiction shows us human beings in their relations not with one another, but with a thing, a monster, an alien, a plague, or a form of society, and while it is true that a society is a human thing, the aspects of it which engage these writers can be validly treated as impersonal. The general point is well put by Edmund Crispin, among other things a leading British commentator on science fiction, in his observation that

the characters in a science fiction story are usually treated rather as representatives of their species than as individuals in their own right. They are matchstick men and matchstick women, for the reason that if they were not, the anthropocentric habit of our culture would cause us, in reading, to give altogether too much attention to them and altogether too little to the non-human forces which constitute the important remainder of the *dramatis personae*. Where an ordinary novel or short story resembles portraiture or at widest the domestic interior, science fiction offers the less cosy satisfaction of a landscape with figures; to ask that these distant manikins be shown in as much detail as the subject of a portrait is evidently to ask the impossible.

This is perhaps partisan in tone, but it does indicate a scale of priorities which operates throughout the medium and which, of course, is open to objection, though this is not often based on much more than an expectation that science fiction should treat the future as fiction of the main stream treats the present, an expectation bound to be defeated.

We have moved some apparent distance from Mitchell Courtenay and his job with Fowler Schocken Associates. True to prescription, Mitchell is a generic kind of person, acquiescent in the earlier stages and thus able to provide denigrations of his society unconsciously and from within. It is through him that we learn of the development of

advertising "from the simple handmaiden task of selling already manufactured goods to its present role of creating industries and redesigning a world's folkways to meet the needs of commerce"; through Mitchell we are progressively acquainted with a utopia of the comic-inferno type built on a complex of assumptions. This is not merely a world in which the advertiser is king, it also combines luxury with scarcity, fantastic gadgetry with an absence of fuel whereby Fowler Schocken runs a pedal-Cadillac, all manner of drinks and chewing gums with an extreme shortage of protein foods. To this extent, it enacts a remark of George Orwell's to the effect that luxuries are on the way to becoming less expensive and easier to obtain than necessities.*
This future America of 800 million people has top-level executives living in tiny two-room apartments and clerical workers occupying single stairs, separated by grilles that lift automatically at getting-up time, in the large office blocks. Here as much as anywhere else that science-fictional uneasiness appears, attaching itself to an existent or incipient neurosis about overcrowded streets and buildings as well as to the rational fear of global overpopulation. The social picture resulting from all this is filled in with remarkable completeness: the foulness of the atmosphere which shuts off the open air as a normal element, the disappearance of poetry that follows the immense expansion of verbal outlets via copywriting, and such splendid iso-

---

* The reference is to Chapter V of *The Road to Wigan Pier*. Chapter XII of the same work, incidentally, contains about the best discussion of the machine age and its future that I have seen. It not only throws off dozens of suggestions that would be of use to any science-fiction writer in search of a theme, it also provides a trenchant critique of innumerable existing stories written since the book appeared (1937). In fact, this chapter gives us a fresh cause of dissatisfaction with *Nineteen Eighty-Four*, which instead of being the remote nightmare it is could have been the savage *short-range* admonitory satire on political forces that Orwell had it in him to write and that nobody since has even looked like tackling.

lated touches as Mitchell's visit to the Metropolitan Museum of Art. He doesn't go much for religion, partly because a rival agency is covering that, but there is a "grave, ennobling air about the grand old masterpieces in the Met" that gives him "a feeling of peace and reverence." This he is able to glut to the full by contemplating a "big, late-period" effort, "I Dreamed I was Ice-Fishing in my Maidenform Bra." One point about this last stroke is that, like some in "The Midas Plague," it connects only generally with the initial assumptions, not specifically with actual current trends. Such elements, free from any loading of significance, are combined with others that concretise some familiar and vague nightmares about the ruthlessness of large combines and the various possibilities of violence increasing to the point where it becomes institutionalised: industrial feuds are legal if officially notified and "there are still bloodstains on the steps of the General Post Office where Western Union and American Railway Express fought it out for the mail contract."

After due advantage has been taken of Mitchell's vantage-point as a hypnotised supporter of the system, and of the comic possibilities of his considering himself a free critical intelligence within it, he is made to change sides. This justifiable unoriginality is brought about not through any spontaneous conversion, but as a delayed result of personal suffering and danger; with the same lack of optimism as is perceptible in Bradbury's treatment of Montag, Mitchell does not begin to hate his society until after it has begun to hate him. In this case it is long after: Mitchell is kidnapped by a rival's trick and sent to a nasty labour camp full of uncultured and violent consumers, and here the revolutionary movement makes contact with him, but he uses it for his own ends rather than becoming a part of it, escaping finally to a Venus uncontaminated by Fowler

Schocken and his friends from an Earth that is still largely under the sway of the old régime. The closing scenes, on which I suspect the hand of Kornbluth lies heavy, offer little but adequate excitement and are not altogether a conclusion to the issues raised in the opening chapters. To provide a solution to these is not what would be expected from Pohl, who like the best of his colleagues is far more concerned to state, with as much elaboration as possible, "the case against tomorrow" than to suggest any straightforward mitigations. Thus the ending of "The Midas Plague," in which the production pipeline is bent into a circle, takes place on a different level of probability from the rest of the story, providing a criticism of the problem rather than its resolution. Perhaps I should explain here that when I said in an earlier section that the activist temper of science fiction was reassuring, I was making a political remark, not suggesting that literary merit is signified or promised by a readiness to portray authoritarianism overthrown by the pure in heart. And in fairness it must be admitted that while some science-fiction revolutionaries are pallid do-gooders unlikely to improve very much on their opponents' policies, enough of them to matter are people hitting out in order to survive or even looking for a place to hide.

The Space Merchants, clearly, is an admonitory satire on certain aspects of our own society, mainly economic, but it is not only that. It does not simply show the already impending consequences of the growth of industrial and commercial power, and it does more than simply satirise or criticise existing habits in the advertising profession, though to its work in this direction it adds some effective parody: Mitchell's handout on the Venus pioneers is a capsule anthology of the ordinary-guy approach, the reverence for experts combined with hostility, the down-to-earth idioms and grammar, the comradely seriousness. Beyond all this, the book seems to be interested in the future as such, to inquire what might result from turns of events that are possible and are not invalidated by being unlikely, to confront men and women with a thing, as I put it, which may put them into a situation without precedent in our experience. That situation, both in this novel and in science fiction as a whole, will be an uncomfortable one by our standards, and it may be used to subject human beings to a kind of insecurity that is both new in itself and novel in the sense that it renders general and public what in the present context is only piecemeal and private. I am not arguing that science fiction primarily exists to allegorise or concretise our own variegated insecurities, for this too would be to undervalue its concern with the future and to reduce it (if "reduce" is the term) to a mere modernistic variation on what Shakespeare used to be taken, and for all I know still is taken, as doing in his Roman plays. Such a reading would also leave out of account an important use made by science fiction of its diverse and massive threats to security or comfort: to show humanity in a disadvantageous light, whether consumed by vanity over its pedal-Cadillacs or finding itself morally outclassed by tentacled aliens. I cannot quite agree with Edmund Crispin that this tendency to deflate *homo sapiens* is a prime reason for the only slowly decreasing unpopularity of the medium among the otherwise intelligent—lack of acquaintance strikes me as more important— but there is no doubt that the deflating aspect is real and, if it matters, intentional. We shall see it at work in the next section in a different kind of story, that in which the thing or threat has no social implications. The science-fiction utopia, political or economic, has a kind of relevance which no other sub-category can match, attracts some of the best minds in the field, and incidentally can perform a valuable introductory service for those who blench at the sight of a BEM; but it is a difficult form, often revealing a damagingly simple scale of values and taxing its authors' invention to the point where a cops-and-robbers interest may fill the picture after the first few chapters. Even *The Space Merchants* relies, as it goes on, more and more heavily upon Kornbluthian elements—there is a quite gratuitous scene with a female sadistic maniac who totes a sharpened knitting needle. Anyway, no worthy successor to it has come along in the half-dozen years since it was published, and meanwhile many an addict must have heaved a sigh for some fearful menace of the old-fashioned type, lethal instead of merely undesirable, and originating on Mars, not Madison Avenue. The supply of these is beginning to run thin, and this is to be regretted, for just as some listeners will find that the Modern Jazz Quartet surpasses Louis Armstrong's Hot Five in everything but immediacy, so certain kinds of readers will respond to a really gutty cosmic disaster in a way that no utopia, however inventive and witty, can quite match. Often, I think that part—and I mean part—of the attraction of science fiction lies in the fact that it provides a field which, while not actually repugnant to sense and decency, allows us to doff that mental and moral best behaviour with which we feel we have to treat George Eliot and James and Faulkner, and frolic like badly brought-up children among the mobile jellyfishes and unstable atomic piles.

VI · PROSPECTS ▶

As I suggested earlier, it would be a mistake to look for any straightforward correlation between the merit or seriousness or readability of a science-fiction story and the degree of its concern with political or economic man. Work that for the sake of convenience I will describe as good has been done with situations that cannot be connected with our own by any process of extrapolation or direct analogy. This certainly applies to a category of what seems to be lessening popularity, the cosmic-disaster story. In the past, a huge variety of these has been imagined, from clouds of lethal gas a couple of light-years across to birds from outer space that turn up to hatch out their chicks, the eggs being the solar planets, including our own. Nowadays such interventions have been replaced by permanent possibilities that lie, as it were, within the system. A great swingeing plague is one favourite stratagem, the main centre of interest usually being the aftermath of the disaster, with its problems of salvage and restoration, rather than the more immediate questions of the progressive disintegration of society and the human effects of this. One such piece which does canvass these matters is an already-mentioned novel by John Christopher, *The Death of Grass*—in the United States *No Blade of Grass*. The plague here, the result of a mutating virus, attacks not merely herbage but all the *gramineae*, including corn, wheat, and rice. We are shown a couple of English families struggling from London to Northumberland, where some-body's brother happens to have an impregnable potato farm, and on the way gradually losing all the civilised qualities they have dedicated themselves to preserve, so that the new start they keep talking about is doomed before it begins: they have to shoot the brother to get into his farm, and consider this no more than regrettable. Thus some sort of theorem about human nature is unpretenti-ously enacted, with a rider saying that compromise is both inevitable and destructive, and I mention it here because it fulfils one possibility of science fiction as a literary mode: as a forum, if not a podium, for the discussion of such topics as what happens when our society breaks down. At any rate, no other outlet is available; removal to the time of the Black Death will not show us our society any more than will a geographical shift to some Middle Eastern hell-hole. Once more, I am not saying that these interests are any indication of moral or literary blessedness, but I do not feel that they are totally irreconcilable with either.

The Death of Grass and its analogues clearly propose an inquiry of sorts into things human; some stories of the same cosmic-disaster kind do not. The most famous of these is a story by Philip Latham, "The Xi Effect." This is the name given to the disturbances in our universe caused by local fluctuations "in a vastly higher order of space-time or 'Xi space.'" Usually these will do no more than send the Andromeda nebula towards Earth at 300 km. a second instead of away from it, which is where it should be going. Just now and then, however, these local variations become severe, on the occasion in question reducing the diameter of our universe to about one-ten-thousandth of an inch. It is meaningful to talk in these terms because the wave lengths of electromagnetic radiation remain constant and indeed provide the investigators with their evidence of what is happening. Before the end, the optical spectrum is affected and, as apparent preliminary to the volume of our own space becoming zero instead of infinitesimal, vision itself breaks down. The final scene, in the Los Angeles Coliseum, is apocalyptic:

Gradually he became aware of some change in the aspect of the coliseum itself; there seemed to be a soft waviness spreading everywhere, warping some portions of the scene but leaving others untouched, like gelatine melting and flowing down a photographic plate. . . . The tiers of seats kept blurring and shimmering as if the light were coming from a great distance through layers of heated air.

With a sickening sensation he perceived that the distortion in space-time was beginning to affect objects right around him. The faces were undergoing some subtle alteration, noticeable particularly in the irregular position of the mouth with respect to the nose and eyes together with an apparent thickening and bending of the jaw and forehead, such as he had once seen in patients whose bony structure had undergone prolonged softening from osteitis deformans.

Throughout this climactic episode, scientific and technological images are cleverly used to give a kind of clinical authority and precision to these untoward phenomena, and if the hero's "sickening sensation" is a sad lurch into cliché, what follows is appropriately couched in the dry, unexcited language of a medical textbook, and recalls the deliberate lack of sensationalism in the choice of title. In general, this is a thoroughly scientific piece of science fiction in the older vein, with factual background material inserted to reassure or impress the lay reader and titillate, though perhaps not persuade, the technically trained. Apart from a bit of parenthetical satire on the sort of person who expects the astronomers and physicists to get the universe expanding again, the entire interest of the story is in its initial assumption and the way in which this is progressively revealed and developed. Such power as all this has is quite different from that of ordinary fiction and drama: at no point are we invited to make comparisons with our own situation and concerns or to revalue our own experience. Instead, the story treats as real what in any other context could only be a fancy or a nightmare. More widely considered, "The Xi Effect" is an obvious example, not only of scientific science fiction but of concentration upon idea. The business about Xi space and its effects in our universe occupies the position given in ordinary fiction to matters of human situation or character; in this sense it is the hero of the story. *Idea as hero* is the basis of a great deal of science fiction, corresponding to what Edmund Crispin in another of his incarnations has called the *plot as hero* type of detective story, that traditional category in which the circumstances of the crime determine the process of its explanation and thus furnish the entire structure of the narrative. This primacy of idea means that a good science-fiction story of this kind will sound good in paraphrase, and in this direction lies some support to the plea that stylistic adequacy is all one need demand from examples of the idea-category, which is not a vehicle for the verbal imagination. I might broaden the notion of idea as hero by pointing out that an idea of scientific interest, or even of scientific respectability, is no requirement, provided as always that conceivability is not outraged. One such instance is Damon Knight's story "Four in One," in which four interstellar explorers literally stumble into a large jellyfish-like creature that engulfs them in the traditional way, but keeps their personalities intact and in telepathic communication. It transpires that their joint body can be modified by mental effort, and after a struggle that is internecine in a new sense, the two more personable individuals refashion themselves in human shape, while retaining their lately acquired powers. One can extract from this a generalisation about the limitations of the scale whereby mankind regards itself as the summit of evolution, but this is only what one might say afterwards, as it were; it is not what the story is about. What we have here, in fact, is the development of a novelty without any of those social or psychological implications which arguably emerge from the work of writers like Pohl and Sheckley, and to that degree "Four in One" could be called an example of *pure* science fiction, provided that this label were understood as making no assertion about the prominence given to actual science. This category is obviously the most forbidding to the neophyte, in that it offers nothing to recognise.

The science fiction of idea has produced many of the best stories in the medium, but it has an important associated weakness. An idea that will comfortably fill out a few thousand words will not do for a novel, or rather there will be an attempt to make it do by various kinds of padding. This can happen even when idea is not primary, as in the later episodes of *The Space Merchants* and in Pohl's single novel, *Slave Ship*, in which what are virtually two short stories, one about animal communication, the other about undersea warfare between 40,000-ton submarines, and both good, are bundled into one frame along with a lot of adventure stuff about a lukewarm war between the United States and the adherents of a new Oriental religion. Similarly, James Blish's *A Case of Conscience* breaks apart in the middle, and one notes that the first and far superior half, dealing with a literally satanic utopia, was published earlier as a long story complete in itself.

The economics of science-fiction writing are obviously important here, demanding as they do a huge output in a medium that calls for a sustained flow of novelties; it is no wonder if some of these get inflated to book-length. One hopes that as the audience for science fiction increases, and with it the authors' remunerations, there will be less of this forced expansion, but I cannot foresee any change in the basic fact that this is a short-story or at any rate a long-story mode, with hundreds of successes in these forms as against a bare couple of dozen in the novel. These are commonly the result of a writer having come up with an idea, in my special sense, that is not exhausted in a single demonstration; one thinks, for instance, of Ward Moore's *Bring the Jubilee*, which takes us on a tour of a powerful and prosperous Confederate States of America and a penurious, backward, agricultural United States. The hero, a military historian, gets a time-machine built and goes back to check on his theories about the Southern victory at Gettysburg. His appearance on the field disconcerts an advanced element of General Lee's troops to the point where they refuse to advance and occupy a vital height. Thus the world we know is set in train, with the hero trapped in its 1860's, for the scuffle his presence precipitates leads to the death of a Confederate officer who was later to have fathered the man who put up the money for the time-machine.

Another type of idea that gives scope for prolonged and apposite development involves alien worlds of outlandish chemistry or biology, the delineation of which presumably appeals to some adult, or nearly adult, version of that interest that induces children to draw elaborate maps of imaginary islands. Hal Clement's novel *Mission of Gravity*, treating of a world where that force is many times greater than on Earth, is a case in point, though the narrative pressure of such inventions is likely, as it is here, to be weak. Even *A Case of Conscience*, which is not idea science fiction, has a six-page appendix in the form of a planetary survey report, all of it significantly irrelevant to the theme of the novel. It seems that this particular kind of exercise of the imagination is an important interest of the science-fiction writer, and to look for its presence, in a rather different form, in the socially oriented utopias of a Pohl or a Sheckley, goes as far to explain what kind of activity they represent as any talk about satire or extrapolation. Without some degree of that interest, I think it safe to say that nobody would set about becoming a writer of science fiction, and since it is by no means a necessary component of ordinary literary inclinations, I should perhaps indulge less hopefully than I do in roseate dreams of half of tomorrow's bright young men fighting to get their stories into *Astounding* and *Galaxy*. But more of that later.

A momentary return to idea science fiction will propel us in a fresh direction. Katherine MacLean's story "Pictures Don't Lie" introduces a space-ship-ful of cordially disposed humanoid aliens approaching Earth on a courtesy visit. Television communication has been established after the apparent discovery that the aliens speed up their transmissions by some factor like 10^4 to avoid the distorting effects of fluctuations in carrier-wave frequency. The ship eventually signals that it has landed, but the carefully prepared airfield is empty. The broadcast continues:

"Radar shows no buildings or civilisation near. The atmosphere around us registers as thick as glue. Tremendous gas pressure, low gravity, no light at all. You didn't describe it like this. . . . This isn't some kind of trick, is it? . . . If it is a trick, we are prepared to repel attack. . . . A half-circle of cliffs around the horizon. A wide muddy lake swarming with swimming things . . . strange white foliage all around the ship and incredibly huge, pulpy monsters attacking and eating each other on all sides. We almost landed in the lake, right on the soft edge. The mud can't hold the ship's weight. . . . *Where are you? Answer if possible! We are sinking! Where are you?*"

The reader is now in possession of all the facts needed to determine what has happened to the aliens, and I hope not to be pointing out the obvious if I explain that the clue is in the apparent speeding-up of their television broadcasts. They don't speed them up, which means, for instance, that when they walk around their space-ship they can change direction in something of the order of one-ten-thousandth of a second while moving at 30,000 miles an hour. No humanoid frame could stand that, unless its mass were very tiny. The aliens, then, are on the airfield all right, but their space-ship is sinking into a muddy heelprint or whatever. Apart from the effects of awe and amazement produced by the description of the pulpy monsters and so on, what we have here is a strong puzzle interest that is widespread in science fiction as a minor aspect and not uncommonly central, as in this case. I have already mentioned the biological puzzle—problems of determining an alien life-cycle and the like—as an important sub-category; another involves the question of finding the weak point in some apparently invulnerable monster or hostile alien or badly behaved human artifact of the robot sort. The solutions to these may be progressively revealed rather than shown as deduceable, but they need not be, and "Pictures Don't Lie" is not an isolated example of the approach that offers what are valid clues, even if they are only seen as such in retrospect. Although interests of this kind can hardly be classed among the most lofty, it seems legitimate to call them as literary as any other. Certainly science fiction appears to be on the point of taking over some of the functions of the traditional detective story, currently I believe in grave disrepair, though with a large audience, in England at any rate, nurturing itself on reprints and the more problem-posing kind of thriller. I cannot believe that the Anglican parson and the Oxford classics don, those alleged archetypes of the Agatha Christie fan, would bring themselves to look through the files of *Astounding Science Fiction* in search of a story like Isaac Asimov's "Little Lost Robot," but they would be the losers by their reluctance, for the science-fiction deduction problem, while to some tastes inferior to the detective story in its weaker connections with the world we know, is superior to that tiny motive-means-opportunity system in its range of both problems set and kinds of answer proposed.

To take the commercial aspect: some partial merger between the publics of the two modes does seem eventually possible, as Anthony Boucher, the most level-headed of science-fiction commentators, foresaw some years ago. I have already mentioned the tendency of the more full-time writers to have a foot in both camps: Boucher himself doubles as the whodunit reviewer of the New York *Times*, and although I cannot personally confirm his assertion that science-fiction elements have recently become perceptible in some detective stories, the opposite process is clearly under way. A recent story by Poul Anderson, "The Martian Crown Jewels," gives us a brilliantly clever and inventive synthesis of the two media, with a Martian detective called Syaloch who affects a *tirstokr* cap, a locked-space-ship problem, and a completely fair presentation of clues ingeniously disguised as technological patter. Even the most hardened Baker Street Irregular would be captivated by this story—if he ever learnt of its existence. Elsewhere, science fiction has been combined with what we are accustomed to distinguish as thriller or mystery ingredients rather than specifically deductive ones. All of these make

some appearance in Chad Oliver's novel *Shadows in the
Sun*. The problem here is why a small town in Texas consists entirely of recently arrived inhabitants and why these
are all too average to be believable. This is soon explained
—the hero boards a flying saucer on page 27—but the
first three chapters are stuffed with 'tec tricks of presentation and style, from verbless sentences and sinister single-
sentence paragraphs ("He was afraid to go out" or "He
had to know") to the image of the hero, who is an anthro-
pologist but tough—the ordinary science-fiction hero needs
no such apology for his learning. This chap

was a big man, standing a shade under six feet and pushing
two hundred pounds. His brown eyes were shrewd and steady.
He was dressed in the local uniform—khaki shirt and trousers,
capped with a warped, wide-brimmed hat at one end and
cowboy boots at the other. His Ph.D. didn't show, and he didn't
look like the kind of a man who had often been frightened,

and as you might expect he soon takes up with Cynthia,
who although fresh off the flying saucer makes good
Martinis and is cool and slim and sets the hero's stomach
feeling tight. These are recognisable as importations into
science fiction, which avoids that particular kind of cheap-
jack stuff and indeed deserves a small round of applause
for not trying to expand its audience by concessions to
salacity. A less inane (and more recent) example of attempted hybridisation is Richard Matheson's *A Stir of
Echoes*, described on the wrapper simply as "a novel of
menace" but in fact fusing science-fiction and 'tec elements
with some show of wholeheartedness to produce a murder
mystery with telepathic clues. The ability of a literary mode
to expand into others is often taken as a sign of vitality,
and it is true that between them fantasy and science fiction
have gobbled up most of what was left of the horror story

without much injury, but I cannot feel that the injection of these thriller ingredients is likely to lead to much beyond blurring and dilution. It is not by capturing more territory that science fiction will improve itself, but by consolidating what it already has.

Such internal reconstruction would do well to start with an attempt to bring sexual matters into better focus. Going easy on the puritanism would be a commendable resolve, and so would a decision to drop sex altogether where it is not essential rather than to decorate a planetary survey or alien invasion with a perfunctory love interest presented in terms borrowed from the tough school or the novelette. What will certainly not do is any notion of turning out a science-fiction love story. In the as yet unlikely event of this being well done, the science fiction part would be blotted out, reduced to irritating background noise—a dozen Venusian swamp-lilies being delivered to the heroine's apartment, and so forth. A recent effort, perhaps harmless in intention but unspeakable in execution, has been made to introduce a women's angle into the field, whereby we are introduced to a gallant little lady pretending to hate her man so that he can push off to Mars without pining for her, and an equally gallant little wife and mother uncomplainingly keeping up the production of tasty and nourishing meals while the hydrogen missiles are landing in the back garden. We can hope for more imaginative treatments than that, but the role of sex in science fiction as a whole seems bound to remain secondary. In the idea type of story it can have almost no place; in the social utopia, it exceeds its warrant if it is much more than illustrative or diversifying, although one would not want to be decisive at what is still an early stage of the medium's development. To view with aplomb the prospect of continuing limitation of sex interest in science fiction is not the same thing as to accept a damaging poverty in it, for we are dealing with a genre, not a literature, and it is unnecessary to chide the *Aeneid*, for instance, on the grounds of its taciturnity about daily life in Augustan Rome. But I quite agree that almost nothing in contemporary science fiction is more calculated to affront the tiro, nor to raise more serious doubts of the medium's ability to come of age, than the horrid lyricism or posturing off-handedness which seem to be the regular procedures for handling these questions.

Similar doubts attend consideration of another, and I suppose related, weakness in the medium as at present conducted: lack of humour and, far more than this, bad attempted humour. There is undoubtedly a kind of priggish pomposity which can afflict even the better writers, enough at times to subvert the moral tendency of what they are saying, and I connect this with the parochial circuit of mutual congratulation, leading in some cases to delusions of grandeur, in which most of them are involved; this as a consequence, I feel, of the history and general circumstances of science fiction itself. As regards simple absence of humour, I like to think I'm as fond of a good laugh as the next man, but I can stand doing without for long periods when reading, having been trained in the Oxford English school, and many of the best science-fiction stories, "The Xi Effect," for example, distil a kind of horror hard to conceive of as harmonising plausibly with anything comic. Some editors in the field, however, seem to have picked up from their reading the notion that humour is a sign of maturity, and compete with one another to fill their pages with stories whose very titles are enough to chill the blood: "The Cerebrative Psittacoid," for instance, or "The Gnurrs Come from the Voodvork

Out.''* There is even a whole mass of writing consecrated to the defeats inflicted on learned but hidebound scientists by a generic Midwestern Paw and Maw of great natural wisdom (alleged) and hideous whimsicality (actual). The British are not guiltless here either: a story called "When Grandfather Flew to the Moon" married the concepts of space travel with traditional—that is, false and folksy— Welsh humour, introducing characters called Llewellyn Time Machine and Auntie Spaceship-Repairs Jones. This outstanding case of unwanted originality won a prize in the London *Observer*'s science-fiction contest, which seems to have been judged by non-addicts; it has been reprinted, with squeals of editorial delight, in a leading American anthology.

However, the picture as a whole is not as grave as this. Humour as a main interest will sometimes work in this medium, provided that the comic notion is a valid science-fiction notion as well. One such example is William Tenn's satire on mediocrity, "Null-P"; others are to be found in the work of Sheckley, Pohl, and Fredric Brown. Beside his contributions to the comic-inferno division in stories like "A Ticket to Tranai," Sheckley has devised a sub-form of his own, the comic problem. In "The Lifeboat Mutiny," two men strive to outwit the mechanical intelligence which controls the boat; it was programmed to meet the needs of an extinct, warlike, reptilian race and is of a

* In case any reader's blood is inadequately chilled by these, I recommend a page-filler series called "Through Time and Space with Ferdinand Feghoot," which for over a year has been appearing in *The Magazine of Fantasy and Science Fiction* (the most highbrow of them all) with horrid regularity. One example offers to explain the pessimism of John Donne's later works by envisaging a time-travel visit to him by Dean Inge, a more recent incumbent of St. Paul's. When James I asks why Donne now spends all his time discussing for whom the bell tolls, Feghoot explains that poets are like that: give 'em an Inge and they take a knell. Oh dear.

verbose, officious disposition. Finally the men sham dead and the lifeboat ejects them into the sea, having read the alien burial service over them. The comedy here arises from the characterisation of the non-human protagonist as it lectures the men on their patriotic duty, offers them food that looks like clay but smells like machine oil, and when they refuse it, threatens them with brain surgery. The solution to the problem, however, does not approach the theorematical neatness and cogency of that propounded in "One Man's Poison." Here, two other but similar men are starving to death in a vast, isolated alien warehouse filled with various outlandish goods, including food, poisonous substances, and a thing called the Super Custom Transport, complete with fuel. The food turns out to be poison and so does the poison, whereupon the men settle down to dine off the Super Custom Transport, which proves to be an animal, and its fuel, which is water. Better than almost any other, this example of the science fiction of pure idea acts as a test case, in that those learned in the medium will at once salute its ingenuity and elegance, while those whose study is but little will complain of not being illuminated, of being offered an unworthy escape from the universe of man and fact, of being presented with a pseudo-question instead of a question.

No easy or direct answer to these objections exists, or at least I cannot readily devise one, but it seems reasonable to stress the point—and this is as good a time as any to do it—that science-fiction interests do not coincide with those of ordinary fiction, though on occasion the two sets will overlap very considerably. The sense of curiosity involved, for instance, is different in each case; science fiction's is more intellectual, if that word can be used without implying any superiority, and it will not always appeal to, though it need not actually deny, that human warmth which we are right to look for in ordinary literature. When, again, we find a science-fiction story convincing, we are invoking standards which, as I have already argued, are to a large degree internal to the system, are arrived at by what one may hope is critical reading within the medium as much as outside it. To notice that popular music uses the same elements of harmony, tone colour, and the rest as serious music, does not lead us to demand that it use them in the same way or else go into liquidation, but when, with this granted, an exhaustive survey shows the popular article to be manifestly inferior in subtlety and importance to the whole classical corpus, the analogy with the status of science fiction is not one I would dispute, though I should like to be offered the chance of disputing it round about the year 1984. I will just prolong my musical image in another direction by observing that an acquaintance with, say, Brahms's C minor symphony and Bizet's C major symphony would not on its own be expected to provide us with any very valuable insight into the later nineteenth-century symphony, or the post-Beethoven symphony, or the symphony. The only way to find out about a subject is to study it, not—forgive the slight hectoring note—to sample it merely.

Humour in science fiction (to return whence I have digressed) is likely to be a main effect only in the idea type, though it would be difficult to disentangle it from serious elements in a comic-inferno story like Pohl's "Midas Plague" or even in *The Space Merchants*, where it appears as a kind of double-edged gaiety. Apart from such as these, there are not many successful instances of out-and-out comic writing in the social category. "Sense from Thought Divide," by Mark Clifton, about a fake swami from Brooklyn who finds to his terror that he really can levitate as he has been pretending for years that he could, is an isolated case of a genuinely comic situation amenable to treatment in this kind of science fiction. Attempts to use humour as an additive or diversion are usually painful, resting upon mechanical notions of comic relief and put into the person of the space-ship's cook, or else reduced to corner-of-the-mouth wisecracking on the part of the skipper, a type fortunately detectable in advance by being described as unshaven and balding. The material of the skipper's jests can occasionally be traced to contemporary novels that are not science fiction, thus indicating an un-flattering view of the fans' reading habits. One corner of the field, not so far mentioned, seems promising for comic cultivation, as for other kinds. This is the category of "high probability," that dealing with the very near future and technological developments already under way. Some stories of this type, the proleptic documentary of primitive space-travel or the first landings on the moon, are perhaps best left serious, but the close-range utopian satire has distinct comic potentialities. These are effectively realised in Kurt Vonnegut's novel *Player Piano*, which is a more withering attack on belongingness and togetherness than any I know in fiction of the main stream.

When science-fiction writers complain of not being taken seriously enough, which is what they are always doing when they are not saying that their readers are the most important part of the community anyway, they have not only themselves to blame. A new volume by Pohl or Sheckley or Arthur Clarke ought, for instance, to be reviewed as general fiction, not tucked away, as one writer has put it, in something called "Spaceman's Realm" between the kiddy section and dog stories. Hostile critics from outside the field will make public utterances upon it revealing a degree of ignorance that would never be tolerated if the subject were Indonesian pottery or Icelandic loan-words in Bantu.

And, alongside the justifiable scepticism of the otherwise intelligent, considerable prejudice remains. That a badly produced pulp magazine can contain adult writing is a lesson not easy to learn, however often it may be spelled out. Those awful covers and crackpot advertisements give an uneasy sense of the gum-chewing adolescents and lower-class laboratory-floor-sweepers who must like the stuff, and I myself fully appreciate the destructive force of an unflattering notion of one's fellow-readers whenever I pick up Jane Austen or D. H. Lawrence. When science fiction does get read at all by non-addicts, it is commonly viewed in the wrong light: as a clue to the obsessions of scientists or of teenagers, as fictionalised speculation among practising physicists and psychologists, as a preview of impending technological development, as actual prophecy. Moreover, he who seems on other evidence to be a human being and yet concerns himself with science fiction is in some quarters viewed with suspicion: is the man really serious, or, alternatively, is he fully rational, isn't this perhaps just a hobby, an eccentric obsession probably connected with a belief in the validity of Rhine's experiments and in flying saucers operated by little green men from Venus, isn't it even a deliberate pose, a piece of intellectual slumming, an affectation of singularity or the adoption of a chic vantage-point from which to enfilade Henry James or deny the existence of Kierkegaard?—a kind of accusation still brought, in Great Britain at any rate, against those who had much of the appearance of intellectuals and yet professed a liking for jazz. A presumptive interest in science fiction can, of course, be any or all of the unworthy things I have catalogued, but it need be none. And I might, with a wholly uncharacteristic touch of malice, warn those whose greatest fear it is to be caught saying "I'm afraid I can't see what these modern fellows are getting at" that among people of undergraduate age, I gather, a liking for science fiction raises hardly any more eyebrows than acquiescence in the fact of Melville or Faulkner.

If the medium, in one way or another, does manage to get itself accepted as a department of serious fiction, one consequence might be a lessening in that hieratic self-importance already noted as all too typical of the contemporary practitioner. Another, one hopes, will involve an increased pressure against the bad writer and a growing concern for style; an expanded audience, with the resultant lightening of economic pressures, would in any case mean that some of the authors might find time to make a revision or two in the original typescript before sending it off to *Galaxy* or *Astounding*. (Year after year of deadline-beating may not have affected Dickens, but then again it may.) What one really wants to see, of course, is not merely a process of self-reform on the part of existing science-fiction authors, but an irruption into the field of a new sort of talent: young writers equally at home in this and in ordinary fiction. One imagines them breaking up that stuffy convention atmosphere, getting rid of the translation machine and the thought form and all the rest of the cliquish jargon, making it unnecessary for poor L. Sprague de Camp to turn out any more essays explaining how stories are written, and, above all, kicking out the cranks who seem bent on getting science fiction a bad name—John Campbell, the editor of *Astounding*, with his psi machine and his interest in reincarnation and his superman theory, Reginald Bretnor and A. E. van Vogt with their conversion to Korzybski's so-called general semantics, L. Ron Hubbard and A. E. van Vogt and John Campbell with the mysterious mental science of dianetics (of one book on this subject, the blurb claims proudly that four of the first fifteen people who read it went insane).

There are signs that the needed invasion from above, or in some cases alongside, is already beginning. The most original and powerful of England's younger novelists, William Golding, is closer to being a writer of science fiction than any earlier figure of comparable stature. His first novel, *Lord of the Flies*, though containing an important episode of fantasy, is an imaginative utopia of moral tendency involving the isolation, for characteristically science-fiction purposes, of a party of young children, marooned without adult company on an uninhabited island. The connection of this strategem and its development with many a pulp treatment of isolation themes is obscured only by the skill and intensity with which Golding handles his material. On another level, it seems clear that he would not object to being classified in some such way, having contributed a kind of science-fantasy novella to a tripartite effort called *Sometime, Never*, his colleagues here being John Wyndham, a good science-fiction writer working inside that professional field, and Mervyn Peake, a bad fantasy writer of maverick status. Although Wyndham's story, the "Consider Her Ways" described earlier, is pitched in a lower imaginative key than the Golding and offers far less in the way of stylistic quality, it registers a higher score for coherence and concision. The trouble about the science-fiction efforts of the writer with real literary gifts is that these may on occasion induce him to stray from the path of thesis and theorem that may be laid down for him by his basic assumption, so that he will pause to conduct irrelevant explorations of character or to luxuriate in the novel possibilities of establishing a sense of time and place in an imaginary context. One result of this will often be to conciliate the non-science-fiction reader into believing that what he is reading is not science fiction and is therefore worthy of serious attention. In otherwise intelligent circles, the term "science fiction" is still often used as an adverse value-judgment,* so that one will hear it said, for instance, that *Nineteen Eighty-Four* is not science fiction; and if this point is pressed by observing that the technological innovation of two-way television is clearly presented by Orwell as the whole means by which Big Brother is able to be watching you, one is likely to be told that all this is only a symbol, as if a symbol could not be actual as well, or as if every journey in space or time were not symbolical too, come to that.

However that may be, it is clear that science fiction, under disguises of various sorts, is creeping day by day into areas formerly thought safe from its inroads. The Alec Guinness film comedy *The Man in the White Suit* would doubtless not have done so well at the hands of the critics if anybody had been rash enough to point out that its propelling device, the discovery of an infinite molecule that can be spun into yarn, is a science-fiction notion of the most brazen sort. The middle-brow Australian novelist Nevil Shute has recently been turning more and more decisively in this direction: his latest book, *On the Beach*, shows us the last weeks of a world perishing under radioactive fall-out. This was handled with a skill notably inferior to that at the disposal of many straight science-fiction writers and perhaps in ignorance of them; but the novel was prominently featured in the general-fiction lists and was even serialized in a popular British Sunday newspaper. Will no one tell them what they read? But to continue with the prospect of highbrow intervention which I have been considering: it has not escaped the notice of top-level addicts that John Updike's recent novel, *The Poorhouse*

* And in middle-brow circles the term is evidently a consumer-deterrent. I have never seen a science-fiction story or serial labelled as such in any periodical outside the field.

Fair, contains strong science-fiction elements while being at the same time a characteristic "intellectual's" novel, though offered to the public only as the latter and of course reviewed as such. This trend is not even as new as all that: I am indebted to a fellow-worker for the information that stories of some science-fiction bias began to appear in periodicals like the *Hudson Review* as much as ten years ago. One such piece, "The NRACP," by George P. Elliott, is worth brief consideration here as typical of highbrow science fiction or near-science-fiction. The title refers to the National Relocation Act: Coloured Peoples, whereby the Negro population are to be brought bit by bit into a huge reserve and slaughtered for their meat. This grisly modern enactment of Swift's "Modest Proposal" scores over its imagined counterpart in *Astounding* by limiting physical horror and concentrating on the feelings of the hero, a public-relations officer attached to the reserve, as he begins to find out what is going on. Further, the locale of the project and the daily life of its administrators are imagined with some delicacy and power. But if this interest, while incidental, is not distracting, the same defence cannot be made of the well-handled, but quite irrelevant, love affair between the hero and his secretary, and a large gap is left in the story by the author's unconcern to explain what has led the American government to take this step and how they hope to go on getting away with it. A science-fiction writer who had won his spurs in the pulps would have gritted his teeth and got down to that one. I do not want to slander the author of "The NRACP," but it is very much as if that dear old justification for any old implausibility or discreditable reticence, "it's a symbol, you see," had flashed through his mind, as it would certainly have been firmly embedded in so many of his readers'. One notes finally, and with sympathetic amusement, the quotation from Auden on the second page of the story, representing the kind of highbrow affidavit which may well become a mark of this stratum of science fiction, and which recalls the bits of culture and difficult writing put up as camouflage by the astute pornographer.

While it is abundantly true, as this sort of story shows, that writers and writing of the main stream have a huge amount to teach their science-fiction counterparts, the benefits from possible increased contact would not all be on the one side. After the grossly inflated and often misconceived claims of the professional propagandists have been laid aside, after it has been agreed that science fiction is not going to engulf the whole of the rest of literature and that we do not need it to teach us science or respect for science or to recruit our young people into the ranks of technology or to break down our resistance to the notion of interplanetary travel, something of value remains. In the first place, one is grateful for the presence of science fiction as a medium in which our society can criticize itself, and sharply. I say nothing here of works not in fictional form, but I find it remarkable that, for example, all main-stream advertising novels that I have read go in for a series of assaults on various aspects of the system, but typically as these affect the worker within that system, and in every case with the reservation that, after the ethical doubts have been gone into, it's a fascinating game that gives you great knowledge of the world. Only in science fiction is the whole concept of advertising attacked and the sense of its fascination used to criticise and ridicule the individual who experiences this sense. In the second place, one is grateful that we have a form of writing which is interested in the future, which is ready, as I put it earlier, to treat as variables what are usually taken to be constants, which is set on tackling those large, general, speculative questions that ordinary fiction so often avoids. This is no less true when all allowance has been made for the shock and pain felt by some when they find these questions answered in a way that does much less than justice to their complexity. Most answers to anything are overwhelmingly likely to be crude, and I cannot bring myself to believe that the most saturating barrage of crude answers really menaces the viability of the sensitive and intelligent answer; if that were the way the world worked, it would long since have stopped working altogether. But perhaps this is just an instance of my own sentimental, science-fictional optimism, so I will go on to observe as coldly as possible that I must not be taken as implying that every writer of science fiction is hopelessly limed in crudity. This is not the stage at which one names names, but at least a dozen current practitioners* seem to me to have attained the status of the sound minor writer whose example brings into existence the figure of real standing. Even if this hope should prove illusory, the suggestion can be made that we could do with more, not less, of that habit of mind which will look beyond the attempted solution of problems already evident to the attempted formulation of problems not yet distinguishable. That is the path which science fiction, in its faltering way, is just beginning to tread, and if it can contrive to go on moving in that direction, it will not only have secured its future, but may make some contribution to the security of our own.

---

* In the event that any non-addicted reader of these pages feels he can face the idea of actually trying some science fiction, his best plan would be, rather than plunging with set teeth into the welter of the magazines, to get hold of volumes of short stories by any of the practitioners mentioned earlier in tones of respect. Many such volumes are easily to be found in paperback, as is the excellent periodical anthology *Star Science Fiction Stories*. The major magazines also put out annual selections in hardback.

INDEX OF NAMES AND TITLES ▶

157